AF408241

Just a Regular Bloke

THE **TED RAY** STORY

ANTHONY SLIDE

Just a Regular Bloke: The Ted Ray Story
© 2023 Anthony Slide. All Rights Reserved.

No part of this book may be reproduced in any form or by any means, electronic, mechanical, digital, photocopying or recording, except for the inclusion in a review, without permission in writing from the publisher.

Published in the USA by:
BearManor Media
4700 Millenia Blvd.
Suite 175 PMB 90497
Orlando, Florida 32839
www.bearmanormedia.com

Hardcover: ISBN 979-8-88771-107-2
Paperback: ISBN 979-8-88771-108-9

Printed in the United States of America.
Book design by Brian Pearce | Red Jacket Press.

Table of Contents

ACKNOWLEDGEMENTS

I am extremely lucky to have had the assistance of Janice Healey, who is a brilliant genealogical researcher, and helped with information on Ted Ray's parents and siblings, and also identified and provided documentation on Andrey Ray's potential biological father.

I would also like to thank John Barber, Chris Emmett, Glenn Mitchell and Marianne Morgan. Professor Stephen J. Nicholson was incredibly helpful in providing information on British stage censorship.

My thanks to Miriam Margolyes and Nigel Rees for discussing *The Betty Witherspoon Show* with me and additional thanks to Nigel Rees for making available his diary entries relating to the program. Petula Clark sent me her remembrances of *Calling All Forces*.

It is wonderful to acknowledge the help from Ted Ray's family — his daughter-in-law Susan Stranks Ray and his grandson Mark Olden. Mark very kindly loaned me some photographs of his grandfather. Other photographs are from London's Cinema Museum (with thanks to Martin Humphries and Ron Grant) and from my own collection. I am most grateful to my partner, Robert Gitt, for scanning these for me.

I must, as always thank Ben Ohmart at BearManor, for his continued support. And also my production editor, Brian Pearce, who always does such a wonderful job.

Introduction

Ted Ray is arguably one of the most difficult to categorize of all legendary 20th Century British comedians. His potential for acting seems, at first glance, somewhat limited, and it is ironic that the one film appearance for which he received much contemporary praise, *Meet Me Tonight* (released in America as *Tonight at 8:30)*, involves a performance as a second-rate impersonation of himself.[1] Ted Ray is basically a stand-up comic, a teller of stories, using his own material and an incredibly quick mind, as proven by later appearances on *Does the Team Think?* Fellow comedian, Bud Flanagan, in fact, referred to Ted Ray's "lightning wit."[2] Another comedian from the same era, "Cheerful" Charlie Chester also wrote that Ted Ray "was perhaps one of the quickest witted of all comedians."[3] At his death, one obituary writer dubbed Ted Ray "the Computer Comedian" because of his amazing ability to ad-lib regardless of the situation. From the 1920s through the 1940s, and perhaps later, he is always on stage accompanied by a violin. And the presence of that "prop" is remindful of three other comedians of the period: Jack Benny in the United States and Vic Oliver and Jimmy Wheeler in the U.K. As Ted Ray joked, "When I was nine I appeared at the Albert Hall and played Rachmaninov. I nearly beat him too."

Just as Jack Benny used his violin in later years as an "added attraction" to his act, rather than a regular part of the entertainment, so did Ted Ray eventually abandon the violin except for special occasions, such as a duet of "Mistakes"[4] with Jimmy Wheeler in the 1950s (wherein Ted Ray is actually wearing evening attire).[5]

The violin that Ted Ray used in later years was gifted to him by Tommy Trinder, and when the former died, his family gave the violin back to Trinder. Not wanting the violin to be sold or used by anyone else, Tommy Trinder arranged that it should, in turn, be given to the museum of the Grand Order of Water Rats.

Aside from the comedy, there was, for decades, music as part of the act, not necessarily from the violin, but in the form of a song. Through the years there doesn't appear to be any particular tune associated with Ted

Ray. In 1932, it was "Lawd, You Made the Night Too Long," a sentimental ballad of a man without a mate, written by Sam M. Lewis and Victor Young, and first recorded by Louis Armstrong. In 1948, it was reported that the song "Can You Look Me in the Eye" had become associated with the comedian. Not exactly a surprise in that its composer and lyricist was Ted Ray, who also recorded the song.[6]

It's interesting that comedy historian John Fisher, writing in his brilliant and definitive book on British comedy, *Funny Way to Be a Hero*, devotes ten pages to Ted Ray, but basically fails to define his comedic style. The best he can suggest is that Ted Ray possessed an adroitness which he was able to transfer from the variety stage to radio. In the former, one skill, that of telling a funny story, complemented the other, that of playing the violin with more than a modicum of skill and panache.

The comedian grew up in Liverpool, but it really is somewhat inaccurate to place him as a member of that large group of comedians associated with the city, and including most notably Ken Dodd,[7] Tommy Handley and Arthur Askey. He was actually born in another Northern city, Wigan, which is the birthplace of one other legendary comedian (and ukulele player), George Formby. (Some might argue that Wigan is also the birthplace of Frank Randle, surely the worst comedian ever to come out of the North of England, but he was actually born in a village called Aspull, close to the city.)

The Liverpool connection is important to Ted Ray, as it is important to all the comedians who grew up there. As fellow comic, Jimmy Jewel, has said,

"Let's face it, apart from Max Miller, the South has never produced any great stand-up comics…The Northerners shared their humour with their audiences. It was a humour of hardship."[8]

Ted Ray once explained,

"Liverpool humour is not so much a type of comedy as a state of mind."[9]

Liverpool natives, or "scousers," as they are known, are certainly not above ridiculing themselves. A great example is the response to the question as to why Jesus wasn't born in Liverpool. The answer: God couldn't find a virgin or three wise men there.

On stage, Ted Ray always managed to seem well-dressed without suggesting a hint of elegance. A jacket and tie was his style but definitely not anything that members of the audience could not afford. Basically, his attire consisted of a lounge suit, as it was once called, a business suit for the masses. His hair was cut short and tidy, perhaps slicked back with some Brylcreem, the British hair styling product, or something similar.

When he first gained any real form of recognition, the comedian had been performing as Nedlo the Gypsy, suitably attired for the role, but once he arrived in London that characterization was dropped, and the Ted Ray persona as it was, and is, known, was quickly created. In reality, it had always been lurking there, waiting to come to the fore.

He was very much Mr. Ordinary on stage. Perhaps in the early years, Ted Ray might have come across as working class. But in the 1930s and later, he was more middle class, in the words of a *Daily Mail* writer, "the typical life and soul of the Rotary meeting who had left a round of golf to share some gags. It was a suburban, sane, businesslike image."[10] And it was an image that he both lived and projected on stage.

As the obituary writer for *The Times* (November 9, 1977) had it "He was, he liked us to believe, simply a man who enjoyed seeing the funny side of life, the pub humourist relaxing with his friends, so to speak. Even the violin, which he could play though he often did not bother to do so, was not allowed to create a difference between him and the average man he liked to impersonate. The corniest of stories and the most elementary of puns were delivered with a zest designed to persuade any audience that he found them entrancingly witty, and under the influence of his clever timing we were persuaded to laugh at him for doing so."

The jokes were sometimes new, but not always. As Ted Ray himself once explained, music hall audiences knew a performer's routine, and it did not necessarily want him to diverge from it. The audience enjoyed knowing what was coming up next. It made for delightful anticipation. Ted Ray was, in the words of the veteran theatrical periodical, *The Era* (December 7, 1932), "a really class comedian."

Generally, Ted Ray found his audience responsive to his humor. He was one of them, devoid of comic clothing and comic make-up. He did not feel particularly adept at dealing with hecklers, although he does provide a good of example in his autobiography:

AUDIENCE MEMBER: When are you going to say something funny?

RESPONSE: When you get a little more intelligence to understand it.

AUDIENCE MEMBER: I can't hear you!

RESPONSE: Don't worry, you're not missing anything!

Ted Ray might have continued entertaining music hall and variety audiences from the 1930s until the 1960s, when the age of the British Music Hall was over. At the end, he might well have had to struggle for engagements in working men's clubs and the like. Happily for the comedian, BBC radio came to his rescue with *Ray's a Laugh*, a series involving opening comedy patter, a domestic scene between Ted Ray and his radio wife, Kitty Bluett, and, finally, an episode of "The Adventures of George the Man with a Conscience." The first season began on April 4th, 1949, and ran for an incredible sixty-five episodes. There were a further eleven seasons, with some changes to the format, and it was not until January 1961 that *Ray's a Laugh* went off the airwaves.

Ted Ray's approach to comedy for radio listeners was one very similar to his approach to audiences from the stage. As one commentator noted, there was "none of [Tony] Hancock's lagubriousness nor Jimmy Edwards' bibulous bluster." Ted Ray was "a palpable life force brimming with good humour and bursting out of the wireless set to grab your attention."[11]

Ted Ray continued to entertain, not so much on stage, but on radio and, from 1955 onwards, on television. And, of course, there was the legendary panel game show, *Does the Team Think?*, on which he was a regular from 1957 through 1976.

Most comedians of Ted Ray's vintage had a catchphrase or a number of catchphrases with which they were associated. Ted Ray didn't have a catchphrase as such that he used in his act on stage. But he did embrace a number of catchphrases that were used in *Ray's a Laugh*. Most related to characters on the show. "If you haven't been to Manchester, you haven't lived," Tommy Trafford would exclaim. Of her latest illness, Mrs. Hoskin would note, "It's agony, Ivy." And the aforementioned Ivy would say of her doctor, the young Dr. 'Ardcastle, "He's loo…ooo…vely." Only "agony, Ivy" would seem to have outlasted the show, but today, even that phrase is forgotten.

One cannot begin to comprehend the familiarity that catchphrases from *Ray's a Laugh* once held for every strata of British society in the late 1940s and early 1950s. At the Royal Film Command Performance of son Andrew Ray's *The Mudlark* in 1950, Ted Ray was presented to King George VI. The latter asked, "Why have you changed your radio show?… Well, you have dropped some of your catchphrases…For instance, what has happened to 'look at your big red conk?" Being told that some housewives objected to this reference to a nose, the King responded, "Pity…I did so look forward to that every week."[12]

Aside from a handful of film appearances and some work in pantomime, Ted Ray for much of his career was never really an adopted character. He was simply himself. It was as if he had struggled to rise to the top in his chosen profession and he saw no reason, or perhaps no interest from others, for his progression elsewhere. He was just a regular bloke — someone you might meet down at the pub, have a few drinks with, and perhaps a laugh. He observed life, and used his act to comment upon its vagaries and eccentricities.

Writing in the *Daily Mirror* in the late 1960s, Matthew Cody summed up Ted Ray's act perfectly as a glimpse of the unheroic, vulnerable element in human kind:

"His is a universe in which corsets are always too tight and false teeth too loose. It is a world in which banana skins await the unwary, in which innocence is a joke, marriage a catastrophe and middle-age a fumbling blunder.

"He may sometimes appear trite, even unlovely. Yet it is lit by a desperate hopefulness without which we might all be lost."[13]

Ted Ray was a stand-up comedian of the old school. He was no Jack Whitehall, no Joe Lycett. He didn't belong to that new breed of comic whose background, upbringing and social position is as much a part of their act and who drop four-letter words with merry abandon. Joe Lycett talks of coming from Birmingham. Jack Whitehall speaks of his youth at public school, growing up in the upper-middle-class London suburb of Putney and shopping at the up-market Waitrose supermarket. Joe Lycett has an accent identifying his birthplace and also, quite frankly, that he is gay, while Jack Whitehall has an accent indicating he was educated at a public school. In a way, it is interesting that Joe Lycett sounds not all similar to another Birmingham-born comedian, Sid Field, whom Ted Ray much admired. Ted Ray doesn't really have an accent suggesting he is from the North of England. His accent is that of everyman, just as his act might be so defined. However, there is a certain authority to his voice, suggesting he knows of what he speaks.

Ted Ray never found it necessary to reference his home town of Wigan in his comedy routine. He tended to avoid humor that might be considered too "racy," but he would often point out, referencing the great British music hall and musical theatre star, George Robey, that there was a place on stage for "honest vulgarity."

In a sense, Ted Ray is different from his contemporaries in that, unlike them, he never pretended that he avoided vulgarity. As he writes in his autobiography,

"My own style of humour has always called for the rather smart joke and I won't attempt to deny that — in a mild sense I hope — I have occasionally employed the slightly *risqué* innuendo. But I do honestly think it is very difficult indeed to lay down a hard and fast rule about what is, and what is not a questionable story. For one thing, it depends mightily on the personality of the man who is putting it over."[14]

What Ted Ray does note is the necessity to try to avoid jokes that might cause pain or embarrassment, such as one dealing with stammering. But, as he points out, through the years what is permissible has changed drastically (perhaps most after his time in 2020). "It's not what he says — it's the nasty way he says it!"

Certainly, comedians had to be careful about whom they joked. In January 1949, Charlie Chester was soundly criticized for an "odorous" joke, a cheap sneer, as one critic had it, about the man "who wanted to sleep in the open and got a job in the police force." Back in 1949, one did not ridicule the police.

In a way, Ted Ray was unique without actually being different from many a stand-up comedian of the past. He didn't rely on anything out-of-the-ordinary in his approach to comedy. There was just Ted Ray being himself, a persona with which audiences felt comfortable.

Without question, Ted Ray was a master storyteller, an expert at under-statement, a stand-up comic who did not use any unnecessary words in delivering a joke. Much of his presentation is borrowed from the music hall, but with a modern technique. He understood that a reliance on gags and stories was OK, but something more was needed, and that was the affection of the audience:

"This was always so in entertainment, but especially in variety. After all, any charm or similar attribute you may have is at the root of your basic appeal; it is often the very thing that makes you 'different,' however good your material may be. For example, two comedians might have exactly the same material. Yet one could fail while the other was a success — simply because one had charm and the ability to 'sell' himself and get himself liked."[15]

"For a variety comedian," said Ted Ray, "the vital turning point in your career comes when audiences greet you in a state of what you might call 'laughter readiness.' Prior to that, all your energies have had to go into overcoming their laughter resistance.

"It can take years. But once they decide to accept you as funny, for the rest of your life they'll start smiling the moment they see you name in the programme. Some agents call it 'The Acceptance Factor.' Personally I've had it from birth."[16]

That may well be true in that Ted Ray was one of those comedians who was as funny offstage as on. At home, he was always "on". "He was always telling a joke," recalls Miriam Margolyes, who worked with him on *The Betty Witherspoon Show*.[17] June Whitfield points out that his funniness offstage made him the first choice for panel games in the 1950s and 1960s. Like Arthur Askey and Eric Morecambe, he had a computer-like brain that allowed him to remember and invent gags on the spur of the moment. Indeed Eric Morecambe himself commented, "Ted Ray was marvelous to meet and talk with because he had a very agile brain. So bright."[18]

Daughter-in-law Susan Ray recalls, "He was continually joking and I know the boys [sons Robin and Andrew] were sometimes really frustrated if trying to make him talk seriously." She adds that at the same time "He was a highly intelligent and deep thinking man and could debate seriously and in some depth on occasions."[19]

The clothing, the average attire, on stage might be important, however much it might seem irrelevant, in a discussion of Ted Ray's appeal. Equally important was the presentation, the obvious charm of the man, the twinkle in the eye and the overwhelming smile. The laughter for one of his gags, he determined, should last seven seconds, and the facial expression during those seven seconds was important. The audience might be laughing at the joke it had just heard, but its collective eyes were fixed on the comedian on stage. Ted Ray discovered that he could avoid blinking during his act. He would gaze steadily at the audience, thus giving a peculiarly personal appeal to his performance.

His timing was impeccable, but his approach to what gives comedy perfection was little more than old-fashioned common sense, and accurate: "Timing? You don't talk while the audience if laughing. It's as simple as that."[20]

Ted Ray might dismiss the importance of an understanding of timing, but one comedian who did learn timing from the master was Peter Sellers, who was heard in early episodes of *Ray's a Laugh*. As his biographer, Roger Lewis (who is no fan of Ted Ray) has written,

"Ray taught Sellers how to pace a line — gave him his rhythms — he also, more tellingly, demonstrated that comic acting could be naturalistic."[21]

Shortly before his death in 1980, Peter Sellers said,

"I learned timing from watching a great comedian who is now dead, God rest his soul, named Ted Ray. I worked on his radio show for about eight years. I was a straight man, and I also worked in vaudeville with him. I could *hear* when he knew the ultimate moment. I mean he'd sling a gag at the audience and they'd laugh. And then he'd know the precise second to speak again to keep them at that level."[22]

Timing was also important in terms of the length of the act. Basically, Ted Ray went on stage for fourteen minutes, did his act and left, with the audience wanting more. As Ken Dodd once commented of Ted Ray and others of his generation, "They didn't have to batter the audience into submission as I do, they could do it. They could score in fourteen minutes and get off." Ken Dodd would take five hours or more to score, but, as his biographer, Louis Barfe, has noted, "he outlived and outgrew that whole era."[23]

Ted Ray might be old-fashioned as a stand-up comedian, but was also very modern in understanding what was necessary to keep his act fresh. As *The Stage* commented in 1952,

"He has not only advanced with the times, but often been in advance of them in style and technique. More than any other contemporary comedian he has been able successfully to combine radio and stage work. He takes great care in the preparation of his various acts. His work is never in bits and pieces; rounded and whole, everything grows from a basic conception."[24]

The performance might not change significantly with age, but the jokes were never stale and generally new from season to season. The acts with which he appeared also changed, but audience appreciation for Ted Ray remained undiminished. Beginning on September 4th, 1950, he was at the London Palladium on a bill which also included Nat King Cole, harmonica player Larry Adler and his partner Paul Draper, and the brilliant American entertainer Will Mahoney, who would play the xylophone using hammers attached to his feet. Just as every review of his act since he first came to London in 1930 had been enthusiastic, so was the latest comment from *The Stage* (September 7, 1950), which announced "One of the best of them all is Ted Ray, with his always funny gags…, his superb timing as in that half-aside, half-mumbled joke at the end of a gag, his violin playing, and his own delicious sense of fun."

A regular bloke with his own delicious sense of fun. That phrase just about sums up Ted Ray for all time.

1. In fact, when presented with the opportunity, , Ted Ray proves himself to be quite a good actor, the only problem being that he was seldom given such an opportunity.

2. Ted Ray, *Raising the Laughs*, Foreword.

3. Charlie Chester. *The Grand Order of Water Rats: A Legend of Laughter*. London: W.H. Allen, 1984.

4. "Mistakes" was supposedly the only piece of music that Jimmy Wheeler could play. Jimmy Wheeler became a television favorite after Ted Ray hit him over the head with a violin. He was signed to a 30,000 pound contract, which ended in February 1958. Eventually, Wheeler decided he was appearing too frequently and cancelled the contract, presumably using his catchphrase, "Aye, aye, that's yer lot!"

5. A short clip of Ted Ray and Jimmy Wheeler can be found on YouTube, and I believe this is from *Midnight Cavalcade*, a charity event at the London Palladium in March 1954, raising money for the Actors Orphanage.

6. Published by Lawrence Wright Music Co.

7. On the first episode of *Audience with Ken Dodd*, the comedian described Ted Ray as one of the greatest stand-ups ever, and a celebrity audience applauded loudly in agreement.

8. Quoted in Shaun Usher, "Ted Ray Dies on the Brink of a Comeback," p. 19.

9. Henry Porter, "Humour Sparkled for Fifty Years," p. 5.

10. Shaun Usher, "Ted Ray Dies on the Brink of a Comeback," p. 19.

11. Nick Smurthwaite, "Radio Sunshine," p. 20.

12. Ted Ray, *Raising the Laughs*, p. 169.

13. Matthew Coady, "The Man Who Survived Vaudeville," p. 17.

14. Ted Ray, *Raising the Laughs*, p. 106.

15. "Comedy and Personality: Ted Ray on Building an Act," p. 1.

16. Denis Norden, *Clips from Life*, p. 273.

17. Anthony Slide interview with Miriam Margolyes, September 5, 2020.

18. Eric Morecambe on *Looks Familiar*, 1978 (Thames Television).

19. Susan Ray, e-mail to Anthony Slide.

20. Quoted in John Fisher, *Funny Way to Be a Hero*, p. 192.

21. Roger Lewis, *The Life and Death of Peter Sellers*, p. 120.

22. Ibid, p. 119.

23. Louis Barfe, *Happiness and Tears: The Ken Dodd Story*, p. 208.

24. *The Stage*, November 6, 1952, p. 6.

CHAPTER ONE

The Early Years

"Wigan," wrote Ted Ray, "is one of the finest little towns in the Kingdom, with some lovely bits of country round it."[1] Having been born there — on November 21st, 1905 — Ted Ray is perhaps a little biased. If anyone does think of Wigan, and most people do not, it is thanks to George Orwell's 1937 novel, *The Road to Wigan Pier*, which provides a bleak account of working class life in the industrial North of England. Wigan, of course, is not on any sea coast and has no pier as such, and nothing remotely as attractive as the amusements to be found on such a pier. That being explained, it must be acknowledged that Wigan does actually have a pier which is in reality a wharf on the Leeds and Liverpool Canal.[2] I suppose in a way a pier does not have to suggest a seaside location. We who laugh at the suggestion of Wigan Pier are actually showing up our ignorance.

Ted Ray's family ties are to Liverpool, and his being born in Wigan is pure happenstance. His father, Charles Olden, was born in Liverpool on August 7th, 1873, and had taken on a lengthy engagement as resident comedian at a local pub in Wigan and he wanted his wife to be with him and have the feeling of security that a house might bring. Olden's concern might also have been that Ted Ray, given the birth name of Charles Olden, was to be his third son, with the first two, Harry Secundar Olden and Thomas W. Olden, both dying in infancy.[3] Mrs. Olden needed not only stability but equally a concerned husband close by.

Mrs. Olden was born Margaret Ellen Kenyon in Oldham on September 15th, 1878, and had worked in the infamous cotton mills of Lancashire, the mainstay of the county's industry, at least as far as its women were concerned. She and Ted Ray's father married in Oldham sometime between January and March 1901.

Charlie Alden

Charles Olden Senior worked under the professional name of Charlie Alden, which he thought sounded better than "Olden." He was a comedian who also entertained his audience with a handful of songs, and he was fairly popular on the minor bills where he was to be found. Playing Barrow-in-Furness in January 1900, Charlie Alden was hailed by the local newspaper as "an up-to-date comedian of exceptional ability."[4] His act went over well in the North of England — the City Varieties, Leeds, in February and September 1900, the People's Palace, St. Helen's in March 1901, etc. — and he was also to be found performing in Ireland, at the Lyric Theatre, Dublin, in March 1900 and the Palace Theatre of Varieties, Cork, that same month. When not playing the halls, Charlie Alden was resident comedian at the Ship Inn in Liverpool, located at the corner of Cannon and Butler Streets in the suburb of Ancoats, twenty or thirty weeks at a time. Here, he would not only tell jokes but also sing five or six songs, many made famous by music hall performer Wilkie Bard (1874-1944), including his best known, "I Want to Sing in Opera" and "The Night Watchman".

Ted Ray describes his father as "a lovable little man with very dark hair and the brightest of blue, twinkling eyes."[5] In private life, he was humorous and quick-witted. From World War One military records, we know him to be of dark complexion and fairly small — only five feet, five inches. Obviously in regard to height, Ted Ray takes after his father.

The father is described by his son as a "born comedian," and much the same description might be applied to Ted Ray. He argues that most children are born comedians and also first-rate, and unintentionally cruel, mimics.

The life as a wife of a travelling small-time comedian was not particularly appealing to his wife, who longed for stability, and so Charlie Alden decided to settle down as the proprietor of a pub — a publican — first as licensee of the Stanley Arms on Watler Street in the town of Chorley, some eight miles north of Wigan, and later of the Bull's Head in the village of Upholland, somewhat closer to Wigan. It was at this time that a sister, Selina Lloyd, was born, less than a year after her brother, on July 23rd, 1906. (In his autobiography, Ted Ray refers to her as Lena, and that is the name by which she was known to the family.)

(A second sister, Jean Margaret, was born in Liverpool on March 10th, 1917. She married railway clerk Kenneth George Arthur on December 26th, 1938. The couple immigrated to the United States, where they became citizens in 1958 and had two children, both born in the U.K. She died in Thousand Oaks, California, on April 16th, 2011.)

What was described as a "major" but unidentified operation led to an extended stay for Mrs. Olden at a Liverpool hospital. Her husband decided to give up the pub and move to Liverpool, renting a small house at 28 Apollo Street in Anfield, and later a larger house at 5 Oakfield Road.[6]

A suburb of Liverpool, Anfield is best known as the home of Liverpool Football Club. At school, Ted Ray had become a proficient footballer, and this led to his being given a trial by Liverpool Football Club. He never played for the main team, but, for one season, he did turn out on a number of occasions for the reserves, playing the position of outside right. After leaving Liverpool Football Club, Ted Ray signed with a junior team, Ainsdale Football Club and played with them for a couple of seasons.

In old age, Ted Ray turned his proficiency at football to good effect when he joined Comics United playing against Blackpool Football Club. The former was comprised of comics appearing at Blackpool theatres in the summer months, and included not only Ted Ray but also Norman Wisdom, Arthur Haynes, Henry Hall, and Jimmy Edwards. Jimmy Jewel and Ben Warriss were joint goalkeepers. The first half was played straight and the second half played for comic effect. If she happened to be in town, Tessie O'Shea would kick off, while Ronnie Ronalde, famous for his imitation of whistling birds, blew the whistle.

With the move to Liverpool, Charlie Alden gave up his music hall career, and became a steward on board various ocean liners, primarily the *Empress of Britain*, sailing from Liverpool to Canada.[7] During World War One, Charlie Alden served as a merchant seaman cabin steward.

Ted Ray attended Anfield Road Council School[8] and later Liverpool Collegiate School on Shaw Street. The latter had been opened by Prime Minister William Gladstone and was initially a fee-paying school until taken over by the city of Liverpool and maintained as a grammar school for boys with a higher educational ability. Arguably, the most famous "old boys" are Ted Ray and Pete Best, who was the original drummer with the Beatles.[9]

Outside of school, the young Ted Ray was an avid "cub" or junior boy scout, enjoying time spent in gymnastics and various other forms of sport with a troop attached to the Richmond Baptist Church in Breck Road. In his autobiography, Ted Ray notes that he made his first public appearance as a cub scout, singing "Pack Up Your Troubles in Your Old Kit Bag" at a church concert, an event recorded in the pages of the *Liverpool Echo*:

"The efforts of Wolf Cub Charlie Olden to help us to smile, smile, smile were frought with great success — we couldn't resist it."[10]

The comedian recalled that he had troubles of his own that summer evening, with the temperature at seventy-five degrees, his face covered in greasepaint, and wearing an army sheepskin coat.

More importantly, as a teenager at the close of World War One, Ted Ray became fascinated with his father's skill at playing the violin and decided to follow in his footsteps. Charlie Alden had always contended that "if you learn the violin, you will always have a living — in your fingers…even if you have to play in the street." As Ted Ray once jokingly commented, "My father — what a fiddler."

Ted Ray recalled that once he was so short of money that he did play the violin on the street, standing for two hours in the doorway of a pub in St. Helen's. He collected four pence. His bus fare there was eight pence.

Ted Ray's father had learned how to play the violin from his father, a professional maker of stained glass church windows, and, indeed, the comedian claims his forebears had played the violin for generations.

An arrangement was made with Ted Ray's first violin teacher, a Madame Pauline (Agnes) Shurrock who owned a music shop and studio on Lower Breck Road in Anfield. She sold him a violin for twenty-one shillings and it, and the music lessons, were paid for on an installment plan involving eighteen pence a week. To help pay for the violin, Ted Ray would earn tips carrying luggage from passengers off the boats at the Landing Stage to Lime Street Station.

The comedian always had fond memories of the Landing Stage and the Pier Head. As he recalled back in 1958, he would stand "within 30 yards or so of the big ships — and dream of going on one of the America-bound liners." A couple of years earlier, he had returned to Liverpool with Kenneth Connor for a radio broadcast and insisted that the two go down to the Landing Stage and Pier:

"This time there was literally no room for those thoughts. A huge barrier had been built there. I could get only so far as the cattle boats. For me that day a beautiful dream had been broken, a romantic illusion smashed."[11]

Ted Ray would begin to visit local music halls on a regular basis, not in the company of his father who was generally working at sea, but rather a plumber from a neighboring street whom the comedian always referred to simply as "Uncle." An "uncle" taking young neighborhood boys on excursions to wherever might seem somewhat suspicious in today's politically correct times, but back then it was apparently perfectly innocent. Ted Ray writes that he was very fond of "Uncle," who had a bristling, black moustache, a foul mouth and an equally foul-smelling pipe.

The pair would sit in the "Gods" or upper balcony of the Empire Music Hall, entertained by Wilkie Bard, a big favorite with both of them, and Albert Whelan (1875-1961), a favorite of "Uncle," an Australian performer who would appear on stage in evening attire and whistling his theme song.[12]

Acts which Ted Ray remembered in later years as liking included Ernie Lotinga (1876-1951), "a really funny revue comedian," and a piano act called "The Two Rascals."

Without "Uncle," but with a school chum, Ted Ray would generally spend Monday evenings at the Olympia Theatre on West Derby Road, where he saw Houdini and a strongman billed as "The Amazing Samson." His first appearance on a legitimate stage was at the Olympia, where he was invited to check that Samson's act was legitimate.[13]

Thanks to a childhood friend, George [Panaylotti] Johnson, the young man begin to play the violin in local dance bands and during intermission at local movie theatres. It was the beginning of a stage career, but not one that Ted Ray was actively pursuing at that time as he was more interested in a career as a professional football player. In 1928, George Johnson married Ted Ray's sister, Selina, and the couple had two children, George K.C. (born 1929) and John B. (born 1933).

Initially, careers on both the stage and the football field were denied him when in April 1926, he sailed for Boston and New York, working as a third-class steward (a position which also included cleaning the toilets). It is ironic that Ted Ray never made it to America as a professional entertainer, and, in fact, is unknown here. The reality was that after the initial novelty had worn off, the young man felt "horribly lonely," as he put it, and was happy to make the return journey back to Liverpool, again as a third-class steward.

He returned to working as a violinist with various small dance bands, playing at various movie theatres. He also joined forces with Harry Wardle and became a singing duo, Wardle and Olden; Harry played the piano and Olden the violin. They played a handful of movie theatres, earning on average ten pounds a week, but the act quickly broke up. Ted Ray wanted to travel further afield for bookings, whereas Harry Wardle did not want to leave the steady job he already had. The parting was an amicable one.

Hugh Neek

Ted Ray made his solo professional appearance at a talent spotting contest organized by the manager of the Palace Cinema, Prescott. He decided it was time for a name change, rejecting "Charlie Olden" as uninteresting. His choice for a new name seemed in retrospect, and probably even at the time, highly strange, an awkward pun — Hugh Neek.

Thankfully, Ted Ray provides a detailed description of the act in his autobiography:

"The act I had prepared for my debut at the Palace was enlivened by a number of these pieces of doggerel [parodies of topics of the day] strung together into a medley. It never occurred to me that anybody could be funny in ordinary clothes and I dressed myself in a queer get-up consisting of a filthy looking old mackintosh, a battered bowler hat and scarf. In the guise of this pretty seedy-looking individual I sang my parodies and then dashed into the wings. I whipped off mac, scarf and hat and reappeared on stage to play the violin, this time being discovered in one of my father's old dinner jackets. I brought the act to a close with a few more verses — again extemporized — to ukulele accompaniment in front of the curtain."[14]

Ted Ray was declared the winner and left with the five shilling prize.

Nedlo, the Gypsy Violinist

A few engagements followed, including one at the New Coliseum, Liverpool. Unbeknownst to Ted Ray, sitting in the audience was E. [Edwin] C. Jazon of the Jazon & Montgomery Management, which served both as an agency and a local theatrical producer. Jazon rejected the name of Hugh Neek and decided that Ted Ray should have a new name, "Nedlo, the Gypsy Violinist," Nedlo being "Olden" spelled backwards. A gypsy bandana tied over the top of the head completed the transformation. Most sources describe Nedlo's appearance as including curtain rings in his ears, attached with elastic, but there are certainly no rings visible in the publicity photograph of Nedlo that appears in Ted Ray's autobiography. There is evidence that at times Nedlo, the Gypsy Violinist, became merely Charles Nedlo.

(There was also a race horse named Nedlo at this time, but no-one seems aware of it, least of all Ted Ray and E.C. Jazon.)

As devised with E.C. Jazon, the new act opened with the comedian standing in the wings and playing a selection of "Songs of Araby." He would walk on stage, with what he hoped was a romantic swagger, and perform pseudo-gypsy-music, such as Ravel's "Tzigane," and then switch to "Turkey in the Straw." The act ended with his dancing around the stage while still playing the violin and concluding with a forward roll. If nothing else, the act demonstrated how musically adroit and physically energetic was the young entertainer.

According to the comedian, he played his last engagement as Hugh Neek at Liverpool's Derby Cinema, and his first as Nedlo, the Gypsy Violinist, the next day at the Gem Cinema on Vescock Street. Nedlo, the Gypsy Violinist, was booked into a Jazon & Montgomery revue titled

On the Panel, the Gem Cinema did not open until August 1926, and so Nedlo's appearance there must have been fairly early in its life. The revue subsequently toured Preston, Halifax, and Huddersfield before opening at the Rotunda, Liverpool (where Jazon & Montgomery had its offices), in August 1927. The star was an obese comedian billed as Tubby Turner (1882-1947), whose stuttering catchphrase was "If it's h-h-hokay with you, it's h-h-hokay with me."

(In July 1927, Nedlo was appearing at the Palais de Luxe, Liverpool, supporting then-child actor Lewis Shaw in a production titled *No Relations*.)

In August of the same year, Nedlo, the Gypsy Violinist, was to be seen in a new revue, *Come Back to Erin*, described as a "revusical,' at the Hippodrome, Nottingham. In October 1927, the show appears to have been retitled *Smiling Irish Eyes*, under which name it was playing the Hippodrome, Belfast. Publicity promised "A story of Ireland and Her People with Romantic Settings, Gems of Music and Brimful of Characteristic Irish Wit." As late as the summer of 1929, Nedlo, the Gypsy Violinist was performing in another Jazon & Montgomery revue, *The Fired Fireman*, which played the Palace, Carlyle, the Hippodrome, Sheffield, the Hippodrome, Leeds, and the Royal Theatre, Bury, among other theatres.

As well as appearing as Nedlo, the Gypsy Violinist, Ted Ray was also required to be a member of the orchestra. What he was not permitted to do was speak or tell gags — that is until he appeared at the Theatre Royal, Sunderland.[15] The audience there was so antagonistic that the leading comedian in the revue refused to go on. Ted Ray agreed to go on in his place, provided he was allowed to tell jokes. This he did, wearing an assortment of hats and using "props" borrowed from other performers. Ted Ray admits that his performance was not exactly a hit, but neither was it a disaster. It helped him realize the importance of there being a bond between the performer and the audience. It also led him to realize that he should no longer be a "dumb" act.

(The audiences in Sunderland were notoriously difficult. So much so that when Ella Shields complained to Nellie Wallace about it, the latter replied, "Yes, Ella, that's why you don't see any children in Sunderland — they eat their young here."[16])

The year was 1929, and Ted Ray determined to change his style completely. At a cinema in Walton, Liverpool, he appeared on stage wearing an ordinary suit, just a regular bloke who might have walked in off the street:

"From the moment I made my entrance I felt a warmth between myself and the audience — a warmth I had never known before. I was one of them. I told my stories casually and intimately as though they were in on the joke. I wore my best lounge suit and, as far as my appearance went, I might have just climbed up on the stage from the front row of the stalls."[17]

It was generally assumed that to make people laugh it was necessary to wear grotesque make-up and funny clothes. Ted Ray proved this assumption to be wrong. As was pointed out, behind the comedian's friendly, boyish countenance lay considerable shrewdness.

With his new act, work was hard to find until a booking came along in March 1930 at the Lyric Theatre, Everton Valley, paying the comedian the princely sum of seven pounds. He shared a dressing room with black-face act, Ben Warriss, who was later to team up with his cousin, Jimmy Jewell[18], and become a popular comedy team. In old age, after the act with Jimmy Jewell ended, Ben Warriss would still appear on stage in blackface, with impersonations of Al Jolson. The star of the show was a comedian named Alf Thomas, who billed himself as "Mrs. Thomas's Favorite Husband."[19] It was Thomas who praised the comedian's delivery and recommended him for his first London engagement, one week at the London Music Hall in Shoreditch. The date was May 1930 and the salary was six pounds a week.

1. Ted Ray, *Raising the Laughs*, p. 17.

2. Wigan Pier is referenced in jokes by George Formby, Sr., and in a song by his son, the better-known George Formby, Jr.

3. Harry Secundar Olden was born in 1904 and died the following year. Thomas W. Olden was born and died in 1910. Neither achieved his first birthday.

4. Quoted in an advertisement from Charlie Alden's agent, Sydney B. Smith of Liverpool, in *The Era*, February 3, 1900, p. 31.

5. Ted Ray, *Raising the Laughs*, p. 13.

6. The house currently has a value of 55,000 pounds.

7. The *Empress of Britain* was renamed the *Montroyal* in 1924, and scrapped in 1930. She should not be confused with the same named liner, which went into service in 1928 and was sunk by German submarines off the coast of Ireland in October 1940.

8. Founded as the Walton-on-the-Hill Board School, its most famous pupil was the formidable and outspoken Labor M.P., Bessie Braddock.

9. Liverpool Collegiate School was partially destroyed by fire in October 1985 and permanently closed two years later.

10. I have searched the pages of the *Liverpool Echo* but I have been unable to locate the reference. The quote is taken from a story in the June 9th, 1956, issue of the newspaper.

11. Robert Hirst, "Ted Ray Looks Back," p. 15.

12. Many years later, Ted Ray was to appear on the same bill as Albert Whelan.

13. "The Amazing Samson" was born Alexander Zass in Vilna, Poland, in 1888. He died in 1962. The highlights of his act involved the bending of steel bars and the breaking of steel chains.

14. Ted Ray, *Raising the Laughs*, p. 54.

15. Sunderland was notorious for the negativity of its audience, particularly at the Sunderland Empire. The Theatre Royal, Sunderland, located on Bedford Street, opened in 1856, was converted to a cinema in 1940, and demolished in 1994.

16. Charlie Chester, *The Grand Order of Water Rats: A Legend of Laughter*, p. 197.

17. Ibid, p. 67.

18. Jimmy Jewell (1909-1995) and Ben Warriss (1909-1993) worked as a double act from 1934-1966

19. Apparently, Alf Thomas was billed as "The Welsh Harry Lauder," and made a few recordings around 1909. In 1910, the National Phonograph Company catalog describes him as "The Welsh Humorist."

CHAPTER TWO

A Decade in Music Hall

Ted Ray came to Music Hall at the end of its era. Music Hall was a Victorian phenomenon, providing affordable entertainment for the masses. Some of the later stars of the Music Hall were still active when Ted Ray entered the profession, and there can be no question that he stood in awe of them. In his autobiography, he writes glowingly of their performances and what he felt to be a member of the profession, appearing on the stages that they once trod. While the tradition of music hall was still alive in the 1930s and 1940s, as Ted Ray rose to the top of his profession, it was more generally described as variety, the British equivalent of the American vaudeville.

Located on Shoreditch High Street, in the East End of London, the London Music Hall had opened in 1856 as the Shoreditch Empire, becoming the London Music Hall in 1896. It was demolished in 1935. "They keep pulling these places down," Ted Ray once joked. "I just wish they'd waited till I finished my act."

As Nedlo the Gypsy Violinist, Ted Ray went on at the London Music Hall. He walked to center stage, lifted his violin, looked at the audience, and said, "This theatre can be emptied in three minutes." Much to his amazement, the audience laughed and continued to laugh at his jokes. He played his violin, sang a song and left the stage. The audience laughter was replaced by applause and shouts for an encore. The theatre manager pushed him back on stage to take another bow. He was told to return to the stage but declined, knowing only too well that he had no more material. Better to leave the audience wanting more.

After the show, Ted Ray returned to the first theatrical boarding house in which he had stayed, and where he lived for quite a while. It was run by a Mrs. Bent, who also provided afternoon tea, and located in the Stoke Newington district of North London.

George Barclay

The next evening, a Tuesday, the stage doorman gave him a card, "Bob Wade — representing George Barclay"

Bob Wade, a gruff, white-haired Irishman, told the comedian that the "governor" George Barclay thought he had something and wanted to see him the next morning.

George Barclay was a legendary, if totally forgotten, theatrical agent, specializing in music hall acts, who also ran the Grand Theatre, Clapham, which had been opened in 1900 by the equally legendary Dan Leno. Since 1919, he had represented another Liverpool comedian, Robb Wilton, and he also represented a hero of Ted Ray, Albert Whelan. Barclay was married to music hall singer and comedienne, Kate Carney, famous for her Cockney songs, such as "Are We to Part Like This, Bill?"

Most agents worked out of offices in London's West End, but George Barclay conducted business at his home, a magnificent Victorian mansion located at 221 Brixton Hill in the South of London. Ted Ray arrived there on a Wednesday morning, and was invited to sign a one year contract, making Barclay his sole representative, with six monthly options.

Of George Barclay, Ted Ray recalled,

"In came a little man, five feet nothing high. He was wearing a cloth cap, and a cigarette was dangling from his mouth…I was to learn that indoors and out he affected his check cap. The cigarette was always in his mouth — and it was invariably a Woodbine [a cheap brand of cigarette favored by the working class]. He never smoked anything else."[1]

Ted Ray stayed with George Barclay through the late 1930s, at which time he signed with Bob Wade, who had joined forces with music hall producer Don Ross and formed the Wade-Ross Agency. In the 1940s, Ted Ray's personal agent was Ronnie Blackie of the C.L. Tucker Agency.

George Barclay died at the age of seventy-five on Sunday, January 30th, 1944. Kate Carney was with him at the end of what had been a marriage that started when she was just sixteen. Until the end it was reported by *The Stage* that he was continuing to give unknown variety turns a chance.

The most momentous decision that George Barclay and Ted Ray made at that meeting involved a name change. Barclay declared that Nedlo sounded like a "ruddy juggler." It did not suit a comedian with a "modern" act such as Ted Ray was presenting. The comedian was ordered to return the next day with a new name. At the theatre that evening, Ted Ray thought and thought and thought, but failed to come up with anything that he liked. He opened up a sporting diary that apparently he always carried around with him, and looked through a list of winners of the Open Golf Championship.

The next day, Ted Ray was back in George Barclay's office with the suggestion that he call himself Bobby Jones. "Too ordinary." In desperation, he suggested Ted Ray, and Barclay responded enthusiastically. It was short, and no matter how small it appeared on the playbill, it could still be seen and read from across the road.

And who was Ted Ray most people might ask today. Edward Rivers John "Ted" Ray (1877-1943) was winner of the British Open golf championship in 1912 and the U.S. Open in 1920. He also captained the British Team in the First Ryder Cup game in 1927. He was at one time a major figure not only in golf (on which he authored two books) but also in all branches of sport. As of 1930, he was not only a golfing champion. He was also a music hall comedian. Ironically, in the 21st Century, both are forgotten to much the same extent.

"Ted Ray," comedian made his first appearance on stage at the Hippodrome, Aldershot,[2] a Hampshire town famous for its links to the British military, in June 1930. He was paid fifteen pounds a week, and his name appeared on the bill below those of the stars, Jimmy James and Rosie Lloyd, younger sister of the legendary music hall star, Marie Lloyd. From Aldershot, he moved on to the Empire Theatre, Southampton, where Ted Ray recalled he received his first press notice: "jokes with his fiddle and his feet and is a very popular turn."[3]

Ted Ray quickly found himself touring the country, his salary now at 25 pounds a week, often billed as a "trick violinist and raconteur." In June 1931, he was at the Argyle Theatre, Birkenhead, and in August of that year, he was playing the Tivoli Theatre, Aberdeen. In December 1932, he was booked into London's Victoria Palace, and *The Star* (December 13, 1932) reported,

"Ted Ray, who is appearing at the Victoria Palace this week, is not likely to forget his debut in non-stop variety. Last night the audience was so insistent that it seemed as though they wanted him to do a non-stop turn on his own for the whole evening. He has a delightful personality, tells some good stories, and fools with his fiddle."

It was the most important engagement so far for the comedian, who shared the bill at the Victoria Palace with Debroy Somers and His Orchestra and Leslie "Hutch" Hutchinson, a black pianist and singer who performed sophisticated songs, and still found time to have an affair with Edwina, the wife of Lord Louis Mountbatten. Debroy Somers' biggest claim to fame is perhaps that he was the first to conduct George Gershwin's "Rhapsody in Blue" in the U.K. in June 1925.

It might seem on the surface that Ted Ray had a relatively easy climb to success in his profession. In reality, it was hard work, and in later years he would brood at how easily a fellow Liverpool comedian, Arthur Askey, had succeeded compared to himself. "I've got to read the morning papers for my act. Arthur doesn't worry about topical material…

"I'm a typical music hall comedian, he is a more gentle comedian who played to a gentle audience at the seaside while I was fighting for my life on the halls in Sunderland.

"Arthur at [the seaside resorts of] Bournemouth or Shanklin was playing to people on holiday. But who goes to Sunderland on holiday? I had 10 minutes to prove myself. I used to walk on and say I didn't want any applause but would they please give me a 10 yards' start?"[4]

Ted Ray's career took a surprising turn, when George Barclay arranged for him to visit South Africa, appearing in a variety show that was seen in theatres between movie screenings. With comedians Jimmy Dunn and Cliff Dee,[5] he sailed on the *R.M.S. Armadale Castle* on Friday, October 3rd, 1930, bound for Natal and Cape Town. It should be noted that South Africa boasted the most developed entertainment industry in sub-Saharan Africa, and was a popular visiting place for British acts, seeking to escape to a sunnier clime. Ted Ray's act went over well, and the comedian was asked to extend the tour for a further six weeks. He turned down the offer, and, with Dunn and Dee, he was back in the U.K. in time for the 1930 pantomime season, carrying 250 pounds in gold coins as payment for his time in South Africa.

The comedian was to return to South Africa in the summer of 1938, this time accompanied by his wife, Sybil, who participated in the act.

George, Gertie and Ted

Ted Ray was not generally associated with any other music hall star, but in the early 1930s, he did tour with Gertoe Gitana and G.H. Elliott, two major names from what might be described as the "golden age" of British Music Hall. Gertie Gitana (1887-1957) is most associated with the audience participation song, "Nellie Dean," Rather like Vera Lynn in World War Two, Gertie Gitana became known as the Forces Sweetheart, thanks to her entertaining the troops in World War One. G.H. Elliott (1882-1962) appeared in blackface and had the somewhat unfortunate sobriquet of "The Chocolate Colored Coon". His best-known song, "Lily of Laguna," was actually performed as a tribute to an earlier music hall star, Eugene Stratton, who had made the song famous. G.H. Elliott came back to fame, or more precisely infamy, in the summer of 2020, when political correctness demanded that his gravestone in the churchyard of St. Margaret's Church, Rottingdean, which identified him as "The Chocolate Colored Coon," had to be encased in a wooden covering.

It was a strange combination, an up-and-coming comedian and two old-timers, but it worked well, and the trio toured, billed as "George, Gertie and Ted," off and on, from 1933 through 1935. After touring in the summer of 1933, previous solo engagements by the cast meant a break until December 26th, 1933, when the show reopened at the Palace Theatre, Blackpool, and then moved on to Birmingham, Leeds, Sunderland, Chester, Liverpool, and Coventry.[6] In September 1933, the show was at the Queen's, Poplar, possibly its first London engagement, and then early in 1934, it played London's Chelsea Palace and the Hackney Empire, followed by the Shepherd's Bush Empire and the Brixton Empress. In October 1934, the trio was performing at the Metropolitan, Edgware Road. The show was produced by Gertie Gitana's husband, Don Ross, who later produced the nostalgia show, *Thanks for the Memory*, and was the first president of the British Music Hall Society. *The Stage* (February 17, 1935) saw the show at the New Theatre, Northampton, and reported that Ted Ray was "to the fore as an amusing and popular comedian." The comedian basically presented stand-up comedy, but he did impersonate G.S. Melvin singing the song with which he was most associated, "Hiking," and he did perform a duet, "I Must Have Fallen for You," with Gertie Gitana. Ted Ray further showed his versatility by contributing additional music and lyrics. From all contemporary accounts, it lived up to its name as "The Happiest Show on the Road".

In his autobiography, Ted Ray writes fondly of Gertie Gitana and G.H. Elliott, describing them as "amongst the most charming and courteous people I have ever met." He added, "To my mind, George Elliott, with his gleaming smile and genuine modesty, is one of the greatest variety artists of his time."[7] Ted Ray's affection for Gertie Gitana is obvious in that he later asked her to be godmother to his son, Robin.

In a review of the show at Hull's Palace Theatre, dated November 25, 1933, the *Hull Daily Mail* concentrated on Gertie Gitana and G.H. Elliott. It noted the presence of Ted Ray, reporting, almost in passing, that "the London 'chiefs' have prophesized a brilliant future." Never was a prophesy more accurate.

Ted Ray, Gertie Gitana, G.H. Elliott, and Don Ross were reunited in 1938 with a show titled *Personality Parade*, which was presented by Gitana and Ross. The former does not seem to have actually appeared on stage. G.H. Elliott was top billed, with Ted Ray in second place along with Chas. "Peanuts" Bohn, making his U.K. debut, and the production was billed as "The Great Anglo-American Revue with 45 Star Artists." Chas

"Peanuts" Bohn is an extremely obscure entertainer, described as a "grand little American comic" whose career in the U.S.A. seems to have extended from 1937 through 1942. In advertising, Ted Ray was described as "one of our most brilliant young comedians."

In London, *Personality Parade* played the Palace Theatre, Chelsea, and the Metropolitan, Edgware Road in October 1938. Its earliest performance was at the Empire Theatre, Birmingham, the previous month, and the show was also seen in September 1938 at the Hippodrome, Portsmouth; in October 1938, it was at the Palace Theatre, Hull and the Liverpool Pavilion; in November 1938, it played the Theatre Royal, Hanley, the Stratford Empire and the Glasgow Empire; and in December of the same year it ended its tour at the Empire, Sunderland.

A critic for *The Stage* saw Ted Ray at the Metopolitan, Edgware Road, and described him as,

"another comedian of considerable merit with a pleasant personality that quickly makes him popular. And his work on the violin and otherwise is well received."

It is quite extraordinary that all of Ted Ray's reviews in the 1930s and 1940s pretty much contain the same commentary, and they are all, without exception, positive.

Holborn Empire

One of the major music hall venues of London in the 1930s was the Holborn Empire, which had opened in 1867 as Weston's Music Hall, and been remodeled and renamed in January 1906. During the period in which Ted Ray appeared there it was operated by Gaumont British Theatres Ltd.

Ted Ray was never actually the headliner at the Holborn Empire, but he was always given featured billing, and as *The Stage* (December 7, 1933) noted, "Ted Ray's patter and violin act is greatly to the liking of patrons." Two years later, on November 28, 1935, *The Stage* described the patter as "rapidly-given" and added that the comedian always added "a touch of his real skill as a violinist." To the critic for *The Era* (September 2, 1937), "There is always something fresh invariably in his fiddling and fooling turn."

Among Ray's appearances at the Holborn Empire in the 1930s were March 1931 and May and June 1939 (with Billy Cotton and His Band), March 1932 (with Jack Hylton and His Boys), May 1932 (with Will Fyffe and Flanagan and Allen), December 1933 (with the Trix Sisters), May 1934 (with Billy Cotton and His Band and Sophie Tucker), January 1935 (with "Hutch" and Will Hay), April 1935 (with Roy Fox and His Band), August 1935 (with the Boswell Sisters), March 1936 (with Max Miller), August 1936 (with Peg-Leg Bates), May 1938 (with Harry Richman and Billy Russell), December 1938 (with Senor Wences and Henry Hall and His Orchestra), and March 1939 (with "Fats" Waller). Virtually, the entire history of variety entertainment is present on those bills with Ted Ray.

Doubtless, Ted Ray would have continued as a regular visitor to the Holborn Empire had it not been a victim of a German bombing raid on the nights of May 11th and 12th 1941. The building was eventually demolished in 1961.

London Palladium

The premiere variety theatre in London, indeed in the entire country remains the London Palladium. Again, Ted Ray was a regular performer here in the 1930s, never top of the bill, but always a welcome adjunct to accompany the star. The comedian made his debut at the London Palladium in March 1932, billed as "A Newcomer." Topping the bill was the largely forgotten Jewish comedian, Harry Green, who was born in New York but settled in London in the 1940s. Ted Ray was third on the bill, following the Palladium Girls with their precision dancing and a couple of acrobats. The comedian thought that his act went over poorly, and when impresario Val Parnell came to talk to him in his dressing room, he feared the worst. Parnell told him that they were changing his "spot" for the second performance. Ted Ray worried that he was replacing the acrobats, but, no, he was now assigned to the second half of the bill, going on second after intermission.

It says much for Harry Green that not only did he not mind Ted Ray's rise in the billing, but also encouraged the younger man.

Those whom Ted Ray went on to support at the London Palladium were both British and American, and included Esther Ralston (an American film actress in Britain to play the female lead in Walter Forde's *Rome Express*) and Will Hay (June 1932), Jack Hylton and His Band (January 1933 and January 1934), Gracie Fields (August 1933 and May 1938), Henry Hall and His Orchestra (August 1934), the Boswell Sisters (July 1935), Josephine Baker (June 1938), and Evelyn Laye (August 1938).

In September 1933, Ted Ray was at the London Palladium, with G. S. Melvin, who would often appear in female attire, singing "I'm Happy When I'm Hiking." *Variety* (September 19, 1933) saw the comedian's act and wrote, most enthusiastically,

"Ted Ray, earlier on the bill, gets over splendidly. Boy has personality, and although his gags have done yeoman service, he has a way of putting them over. Ray can also match a violin with the best of them."

On June 1, 1932, *The Era* reported that the comedian was appearing at both the Holborn Empire and the London Palladium, and that George Barclay had booked him on some sixty tours. "What a ray of sunshine for Variety," commented the newspaper.

In the fall of 1932, Ted Ray was booked by Moss Empires to appear at the Dominion, Tottenham Court Road, but because of a jurisdictional dispute with General Theatres Corporation, that booked the London Palladium, his appearance was cancelled. Moss Empires instead booked him into the Empire Theatre, Birmingham, in November 1932, in a show titled *The Saucy Nineties*, a tribute to old-time songs and dances, headed by Rosie Lloyd.

Standing at the side of the stage on the opening Monday night, the comedian noticed one of the six dancing girls in the show. Her name was Sybil Dorothy Stevens, known as either Sybil or Sib, and Ted Ray plucked up the courage to ask her to come to the cinema on the Wednesday afternoon. He left Birmingham on Sunday for his next engagement at the Hippodrome, Portsmouth, wondering if he would see Sybil again.

He did and a romance blossomed, leading to Ted Ray's marrying Sybil Stevens at the Croydon Registry Office on July 11th, 1933. A dancer named Danny Lipton was best man. The couple rented a small furnished apartment in Mitcham, just south of London, and Sybil was hired to tour with Ted in "George, Gertie and Ted."

Ted would constantly try out his jokes on Sybil and, later, on his children. Sybil, it is reported, would laugh at everything — funny or not. The marriage was basically a happy one, although there were rumors that Ted had affairs through the years.

In his autobiography, Ted Ray links the happiness of his marriage with the sad death of his father. However, the latter did not die until March 1934. He and the comedian's mother were still living at the same Liverpool address which Ted Ray had also called home, 5 Oakfield Road. Charles Olden Senior was buried at Liverpool's West Derby cemetery on August 3, 1934. Ted Ray, who was appearing at the Hackney Empire that week, travelled up north for the funeral. His mother. Margaret, died in June 1941 in Blackburn, Lancashire. She is buried next to her husband.

Ted Ray topped the bill at the Victoria Palace as early as March 1933, sharing headline billing with the long-forgotten Singing Comedians, Reilly and Comfort. The comedian was often billed with on-stage orchestras, such as Harry Roy and His Band at the Birmingham Hippodrome in January 1938, and Alfred Rose and His Orchestra at the Finsbury Park Empire in April 1933. Later, at the Finsbury Park Empire, he was the supporting act to beloved American stars and long-time U.K. residents, Bebe Daniels and Ben Lyon in March 1938, and to cowboy star Tom Mix and His Horse Tony, beginning December 12th of that same year.

A year earlier, at another appearance at the Finsbury Park Empire, *The Stage* (May 27, 1937) had noted "an air of personal enjoyment that enhances the appeal of his gags." A good point to make in that Ted Ray always seemed to be having a good time, and that sense of pleasure also engulfed his audience.

It is an almost impossible task to document all of Ted Ray's variety appearances in the 1930s. He is endlessly busy. In December 1934, he played the Empire Theatre, Penge, and on the same bill was fourteen-year-old Hughie Green, who was a year away from starring on screen as *Midshipman Easy*, and was to go to host a ridiculously popular talent show, *Opportunity Knocks*.[8] In October 1935, he was at the Lewisham Hippodrome, supporting musical comedy star Alice Delysia and Scottish comedian, Will Fyffe, whom Ted Ray always looked upon with great affection, In March 1936, he was at the Brighton Hippodrome, supporting Hollywood matinée idol Ramon Novarro. In his autobiography, Ted Ray notes that on the same bill was dancer, Eddie Ready, who bore a striking resemblance to Novarro. One evening, Ready appeared at the stage door and was attacked by a horde of women who tore his clothes off, thinking he was the Hollywood star. In July 1937, Ted Ray was at the Princess Theatre, Bristol, supporting ventriloquist Arthur Prince. In March 1939, he was at London's Adelphi Theatre, supporting Max Miller, a comedian with a very different style of patter and a penchant for flamboyant and vulgar clothing. In December 1940, he was hailed by *The Stage* as "a welcome visitor," when he supported organist Reginald Foort at the Empire Theatre, Liverpool. He was back at the Empire in September 1944 in the revue, *Gangway*.

Pantomime

Most comedians from Ted Ray's era would spend the Christmas season on stage in that peculiar British institution, the pantomime. Ted Ray was no exception, although his appearances seem to be on a less regular basis.

The December 28th, 1928, edition of the theatrical publication, *The Stage*, contains a report on a production of *Jack and the Beanstalk* at the Opera

House, Southport, which had begun on Boxing Day. In the cast is Chas. Nedlo as King Cobblefeet, and there is no reason to doubt this is Ted Ray making his first appearance in pantomime. "The specially selected company and the staging are excellent, and the pantomime proves to be very entertaining and enjoyable in each of its eleven scenes," reported *The Stage*.

The earliest pantomime in which he appeared as Ted Ray would seem to be *Jack and the Beanstalk* at the South London Streatham Hill Theatre in 1937/1938, with Marie Burke as the principal boy. Billed as "The Great Spectacular Drury Lane Pantomime," *Jack and the Beanstalk* was described by the *Daily Telegraph* as "A lavish production," although it is not clear if that critical praise related to the Drury Lane production or to the one at the Streatham Hill Theatre.

For pantomime engagements, Ted Ray was generally cast as "Buttons" (a role for which he seems a little old) in Don Ross' production of *Cinderella*, in which he would seem first to have appeared at London's Metropolitan, Edgware Road, in the 1939/1940 season. Emile Littler produced *Cinderella* for the 1941/1942 season not at the Prince of Wales Theatre, Birmingham, where his shows were usually featured, but at the Memorial Theatre, Stratford-on-Avon.

A more ambitious production of *Cinderella* opened at London's Stoll Theatre, Kingsway, on December 24, 1942, with an all-star cast, including comedians Nervo and Knox and Naunton and Gold, and with stage star Fay Compton as the principal boy. The *Daily Herald* (December 28, 1942) praised Ted Ray's "wistful waggery." Interestingly, playing Baron Hardup of Stoneybroke Castle was Kenneth Blain, who is best remembered for working with Arthur Askey and writing his most famous number, "The Bee Song." Later productions did not have the same star appeal as the pantomime was presented at the New Theatre, Brighton, in 1945/1946, and the Hippodrome, Brighton, in 1946/1947. For the 1948/1949 season at the Bristol Hippodrome, Ted Ray lived in his trailer-caravan, which he parked on a bombed-out site near the theatre. One night, while the comedian was on stage, the trailer-caravan was burgled.

For a starring appearance in *Aladdin* at the Coventry Hippodrome, opening on Christmas Eve, 1943, Ted Ray donned a dress, and didn't look too good in it, to play Widow Twanky. This was the first time the comedian had worn a dress and played a Dame on stage. "To suddenly appear as Aladdin's old mother is indeed a new experience for him and the audience," reported the Coventry *Standard* (January 1, 1944).

Other comedians of the period, for example Arthur Askey, enjoyed early careers not only on the stage in concert parties and as solo performers, but also on radio and on screen. Ted Ray's career was substantially different in that it was primarily limited, during the years in which he grew in stardom, to the music hall stage and nothing else. It was as if he had struggled to rise to the top in his chosen profession and he saw no reason, or perhaps no interest from others, for his progression elsewhere. More importantly, perhaps, his music hall contracts in the 1930s stipulated that he would not be heard on radio, the fear being that one radio broadcast would throw away an entire year's worth of music hall jokes.

He was once asked to appear in a play with eighteen months work. He responded that eighteen months sounded like a jail sentence.

1. Ted Ray, *Raising the Laughs*, p. 74.

2. The Hippodrome opened in 1913 and was demolished in 1961. Peter Sellers, who was later to be associated with Ted Ray, played there for a week, beginning February 9th, 1948. Sellers played the drums and was a disaster, in part because the orchestra would eat sandwiches while he was on stage and was always four bars behind him.

3. Ted Ray, *Raising the Laughs*, p. 78.

4. Horace Richards, "Ay Thang Yow!"

5. In his autobiography, Ted Ray writes that the only other artists on board the ship were a French double act, Christiane and Duroy. But this would appear to be incorrect, as *The Stage* (October 9, 1930) reports Dunn and Dee on the ship.

6. The show was also seen in Aldershot, Belfast, Bournemouth, Croydon, Derby, Doncaster, Dublin, Edinburgh, Glasgow, Grimsby, Hull, Ipswich, Keighley, Kingston upon Thames, Leeds, Manchester, Morecambe, New Cross, Newcastle, Newport, Northampton, Norwich, Nottingham, Penge, Plymouth, Salford, Sheffield, Southampton, Swansea, and Wolverhampton. A study of the cities in which the trio appeared provides a good record of variety theatres operating in the U.K. at this time.

7. Ted Ray, *Raising the Laughs*, pp. 86-87.

8. A lengthy discussion of Hughie Green's career does not really belong here, but I urge readers to look him up on the internet. The biggest discovery on *Opportunity Knocks* was Les Dawson, who was to work with Ted Ray on the television panel game, *Jokers Wild*.

CHAPTER THREE

Beyond Music Hall

The 1940s began with Ted Ray's continuing what might be described as an onslaught on British music halls, including the Empire Theatre, Edinburgh (January 1940); the Hippodrome (Brighton) in June of 1940, with Carroll Levis and His Discoveries, hosted by Levis;[1] the Empire, Nottingham (February 1940); the Empire Theatre, Liverpool (December 1940), with Reginald Foort topping the bill at the organ; the Edinburgh Empire (January 1940); the Finsbury Park Empire (June 1940) and the Glasgow Empire (January 1941), co-starring with impersonator Florence Desmond; the Kingston Empire, with sophisticated female impersonator Douglas Byng and musical comedy star Harry Welchman; the Glasgow Empire (November 1942), and the Wood Green Empire (April 1943). In June 1940, Ted Ray was featured at the Palace, Manchester, on a music hall bill described as "Youth Takes a Bow." The African-American singer Adelaide Hall was hardly youthful, but perhaps the title described another on the bill, Dick Bentley, an Australian performer who was yet to make his name on radio with Jimmy Edwards in *Take It from Here*.

Beyond Compère

While Ted Ray had performed in a number of shows that were billed as revues, in reality, they were little more than music hall entertainment under what was perhaps assumed to be a more appealing name. His first appearance in what can be described as genuine revue came in 1940 when he was starred in *Beyond Compère*, written by Ronald Frankau, with music by Monte Crick, Conrad Leonard and John Burnaby.

Ronald Frankau (1894-1951), who comes from a fairly illustrious family, was primarily a cabaret entertainer, telling jokes and singing songs accompanied by Monte Crick on the piano. He was notorious for his recordings of saucy numbers, banned by the BBC, which included "Winnie the Worm" and "Everyone's Got Sex Appeal for Someone," which led to his teaming with Tommy Handley under the name of Murgatroyd and Winterbottom. Two years after appearing with Ted Ray, Frankau recorded his best known song, "The Jap and the Wop and the Hun."

Beyond Compère opened at London's Duchess Theatre on March 15th, 1940, with Renée Roberts providing the female lead. Despite its running some 133 performances, Ted Ray makes no mention of it in his autobiography.

"In boisterous contrast to the subtleties of Mr. Frankau," wrote *The Stage* (March 21, 1940), "is the breeze personality of Ted Ray, whose cheery patter, nimble manipulation of the violin and hitherto unsuspected powers of impersonation make him a valuable artist in revue, and quickly confirm his established reputation as a successful comedian of the music-hall stage."

Praising Ted Ray's performance with the violin and his "good jokes," the *Daily Mirror* (March 16, 1940) described the show as "a very bright revue of the sophisticated kind."

A portion was broadcast for the armed forces on April 15th, 1940.

Black Velvet

Ronald Frankau and Ted Ray were reunited in another revue, *Black Velvet*. They did not appear in the original London production, nor in the original touring production, but appear to have been brought in as an effort to enhance the latter.

Produced by George Black, *Black Velvet* had opened at the London Hippodrome on November 14, 1939, and was to run through September 9, 1940. It starred Vic Oliver and Teddy Brown, and also in the cast were Pat Kirkwood and music hall veteran, Alice Lloyd, another of Marie Lloyd's sisters. While still playing on the London stage, a touring production of this "intimate rag," as it was described, opened at the Palace Theatre, Manchester, on March 18, 1940, starring Stanelli,[2] "with his violin and inconsequential chatter."

The revue's concept was that of a mixture of champagne and stout, with popular songs from composers such as Cole Porter. In many respects, Frankau and Ray seem naturals to lead the company, and, of course, Ted Ray had the obligatory violin used by Vic Oliver in London and Stanelli in the initial tour. The new version, with Frankau and Ray, opened in the summer of 1940, and emphasis was placed on their both using their own material. This seems somewhat odd in that the revue was described as an exact replica of that playing at the London Hippodrome.

Black Velvet made return visits to both Coventry and Birmingham. The *Coventry Evening Telegraph* (February 18, 1941) reviewed the show at the New Hippodrome, and wrote that "The cheerful fooling of Ted Ray runs through *Black Velvet* like a backbone, and he vitalises every scene in which he appears." Seeing the show at the Birmingham Hippodrome, the *Birmingham Mail* (April 8, 1941) described it as "a light-hearted piece of frivolity, abounding in funny situations and affording the audience opportunity of participating in the entertainment." A critic from *The Stage* (April 10, 1941) also saw Ted Ray at the Birmingham Hippodrome, and declared him "an able and resourceful comedian."

Ronald Frankau and Ted Ray toured the provinces in *Black Velvet* from 1940 through 1942.

Gangway

In 1944, Ted Ray was touring in a George Black-produced revue, *Gangway*, which was little more than a spectacular version of a music hall bill. There were sketches, such as one written by Val Guest and titled "Panama Tatty" (a parody of the popular musical title, *Panama Hattie*). Ted Ray appeared as the Beachcomber with Jill Manners in the title role. *The Stage* (November 2, 1944) reviewed the production when it played London's Golders Green Hippodrome, and commented,

"In the comic line Ted Ray is in the fore. He is always funny and original. His impressions, for instance, are a little different from anyone else's, particularly in their delivery — there is an air of inconsequence about them."

Gangway had opened at the London Palladium in the summer of 1942, with Ben Lyon and Bebe Daniels, Jimmy Jewell and Ben Warris, and Tommy Trinder. Ted Ray replaced the last, while Vera Lynn was brought in to the Palladium show to replace an ill Bebe Daniels.

Another revue, which was really nothing more than a music hall bill was *Let's Get a Load of This*, in which Ted Ray was featured at the Empire, Edinburgh and the Empire, Glasgow (both July 1943), the Brighton Hippodrome (September 1943), and the Empire Theatre, Newcastle (October 1943), among many others.

To celebrate VE Day, perhaps a little prematurely, Tom Arnold presented a revue titled *We'll Be Seeing You*, starring Ted Ray and "Hutch". The title is presumably based on two popular songs of the period, the American "I'll Be Seeing You" and the Vera Lynn favorite, "We'll Meet Again." It began touring in April 1945 at the Birmingham Hippodrome and the Liverpool Empire, and also played (among others) the Empire Theatre, Nottingham (May), the Empire Theatre, Edinburgh (June), the

Winter Gardens, Morecambe (July), the Coventry Hippodrome (July), the Palace Theatre, Blackpool (July and August), and the Grand Theatre, Derby (September). In London, *We'll Be Seeing You* played the Finsbury Park Empire (May) and the Wood Green Empire and the Hackney Empire (both August). On October 13th, 1945, the revue was seen at the newly-reopened Metropolitan Theatre, Edgware Road, with performances at 6:00 and 8:00 p.m.

Ice Revue

One most out-of-the-ordinary revue-style entertainment in which Ted Ray participated was *Ice Revue*, featuring a group of professional skaters, and the comedian (who was not on skates), which opened at London's Stoll Theatre on October 10th, 1946. The show, directed and staged by Gerald Palmer, featured what was described as the largest ice stage ever seen in Europe, some 2,000 square feet, and starred amateur champion Cecilia College.[3] Ted Ray was described as part of a "cabaret of variety personalities," there to break up the monotony of two hours of ice skating.

Ice Revue returned to the Stoll Theatre in July 1949, rechristened *Ice Vogues*. The principal comic was Richard Hearne, known for his impersonation of Mr. Pastry. Here he appeared briefly on skates and then returned for a "Neapolitan Carnival," without skates. Ted Ray appeared prior to intermission with an interlude from his radio show, *Ray's a Laugh*. "Although appearing without skates the outfit puts on a snappy vaude routine," reported *Variety* (July 27, 1949). The critic of *The Times* (July 16, 1949) noted, "Mr. Ted Ray is there to demonstrate the ease with which a witty man can skate on thin ice without really skating."

Ted Ray made what was announced to be his final appearance in an ice show when he starred in *Holiday on Ice* at the Garrick Theatre, Southport in May 1957.

In March 1945, *Variety* published a listing of weekly salaries earned by British performers on stage. Topping the list were George Formby ($5,200.00), Flanagan and Allen ($4,800.00), Max Miller ($3,200.00), Old Mother Riley ($3,200.00), and Vera Lynn ($3,000.00). Ted Ray was grouped with Wee Georgie Wood, Issy Bonn and Arthur Prince at $700.00 per week. Wilson, Keppel and Betty earned $600.00 a week.[4]

A weekly salary of only $700.00 might seem small for someone as well known, and as popular, as Ted Ray, but it was certainly coming in on a regular basis. Aside from his appearances in revues, the comedian was still working in variety/music hall, for example, a 1948 summer season at the

Grand Theatre, Blackpool, and, of course, he was still to be found on stage at the London Palladium.

For its big summer show in 1949, opening late July, the London Palladium booked Ted Ray, fourth billed, to appear in what seems to be a panoply of stars from the United States, including Frances Langford, headlining, actor Jon Hall, eccentric dancer Cass Daley, and the brilliant Chaz Chase, whose act consisted of his eating anything he could get his teeth into. Ted Ray was actually still appearing in *Ice Vogues* while also working the stage of the Palladium. *Variety* (August 10, 1949) described him as "now almost a resident comedian at this house."

This would certainly appear to be so, with other, previous appearances at the London Palladium worthy of note, and with Ted Ray's supporting various American stars. While audiences obviously flocked to the London Palladium to see the American headliners, that same audience was equally happy to find a British act that it might enjoy as much as the American star(s). And that British act provided the comedy interlude that a show promoting a non-comedian and sometimes non-variety stars would need.

Danny Kaye

The American star who had the most influence on Ted Ray, not so much in terms of his act, but rather his outgoing personality, was Danny Kaye (1911-1987). Ted Ray writes glowingly of the American in his autobiography, of the high regard in which he was held by the Royal Family, and of Kaye's stopping his act in order to introduce the comedian's family seated in a box.

"He was unlike any other comedian of the orthodox kind that we had ever seen," wrote Ted Ray. "He could sing, he could mime, he could act — and above all, he had the spark of comic genius. There was also that wonderful gift of sympathy and pathos — Danny can switch from laughter to tears quicker than anybody I know — and he is intrinsically a very, very funny man."[5]

Danny Kaye and Ted Ray first played the Palladium together in February 1948. According to the *Times*, the latter was the only member of the supporting players who "rises above a dreary and sometimes distasteful mediocrity."[6] The couple reunited in April 1949 on a bill that also included ventriloquist Bobbie Kimber, who fooled audiences into believing he was a woman while actually a man in disguise. The *Daily Herald* (April 12, 1949) reported that Ted Ray received the biggest ovation for an act that also included impersonations of Al Jolson, Jimmy Durante and

Winston Churchill. The last was in the audience one evening and apparently approved of Ray's impersonation of him,

The *Daily Herald* seemed to be trying to incite an Anglo-American dispute as to which star was bigger and better. Its critic, P.L. Mannock, reported that Ted Ray was "a refreshing British contrast to Mr. Kaye's ultra-American methods."

After one of his performance, Danny Kaye asked Ted Ray if he could borrow one of the pieces of Ted Ray soap, which was still rationed at that time. Ted was happy to make the loan, and even happier when Danny Kaye sent him a case of soap on his return to the United States.

Aside from Danny Kaye, Ted Ray also supported Hollywood star Carmen Miranda, along with comedians George and Bert Bernard, in April and May 1948. Prior to opening at the Palladium, the company had played the Finsbury Park Empire in March 1948. (Somehow the notion of Carmen Miranda's playing the Finsbury Park Empire seems ludicrously funny.) In April 1949, Ted Ray appeared with Kathryn Grayson on a bill that also included another (and brilliant) ventriloquist Arthur Worsley. Ted Ray was billed second after the intermission, and immediately prior to Kathryn Grayson's performance.

Of his performance, *The Stage* (April 14, 1949) commented,

"No artist had a heartier reception on Monday, and more thoroughly deserved it than Ted Ray. His quips and gags, most of them entirely new, are put over with a delightful air of nonchalance. As soon as he walks on the stage one feels the grip on his audience, a grip which he never loses."

He does not identify the lady by name, but surely Ted Ray is writing of Kathryn Grayson when he records she ended her first performance by telling the audience, "Ladies and gentleman last night just before I went to sleep I prayed that I would be a big success on my opening here." She paused and then added, "Believe me, I shall have an awful lot to tell God tonight." The audience refrained from booing her off stage, but she was obviously told to forget the comment at the next performance.

Major appearances at the London Palladium did nothing to prevent Ted Ray's appearing on typical music hall bills across the country. He was at the Reading Palace in February 1945, topping the bill alongside veteran music hall star and male impersonator Hetty King. (It must have been exciting for the comedian to know he was appearing with an entertainer who, in the 1910s, had been married to one of the music hall performers he idolized when he was young, Ernie Lottinga.) And he was back again at the Palace, Reading, in January 1948. In July 1947, he was at the Hackney Empire, and in September of the same year, he was at the Shepherd's Bush Empire. In June 1949, Ted Ray topped a lackluster bill at the Finsbury Park Empire, with the performers grouped together as the "Paradise Parade."

The last touring revue in which Ted Ray appeared in the autumn and winter of 1948 was *It's on the Air*, with Henry Hall and His Orchestra, and with Jill Manners, who had worked previously with the comedian, as leading lady. In one sketch, the comedian appeared as a boxer misidentified as a society gentleman. *The Stage* (December 9, 1948), in a somewhat confused and badly written review, reported,

"In this Ted Ray, the chief comedian, wears a moustache and a frock-coat, and shows himself to be as funny in character as he is with violin, chin, and his easy flow of jokes, which appears so casual yet is the product of a highly-developed art. Some of his jesting is so up-to-the-minute that it must be impromptu. 'Can You Look Me in the Eye?' he sings. There is certainly a mischievous look in his when he says he hope his latest song will sweep the country."

"Can You Look Me in the Eye," published by Lawrence Wright Music Publishing, is one of many songs for which Ted Ray wrote both the music and lyrics. He was certainly not shy about promoting his own work, not just on stage but also on the BBC. "Can You Look Me in the Eye" was heard on the BBC sung by the comedian and also by the Five Smith Brothers (billed as "Mr. and Mrs. Smith's 5 Little Boys") on a show titled *Up the Pole* (which starred Jimmy Jewel and Ben Warriss).[7]

In the late 1930s, Ted Ray and his family moved into a new house, where the comedian was to live until his death. Previously, the family had been residing in an apartment in Barnes, South of the River. The house was located at 11 Belgrave Gardens, Southgate, in the London suburb of Enfield. The comedian put down a 300 pound deposit on the property, which left him with just fifteen pounds in the bank. In 1952, he boasted to the left-wing *Daily Herald* that he had a two-car garage, an acre of garden and a daily help named Mrs. Wheeler.[8] Readers must have been impressed.

He didn't mention that the detached, corner property, named "Arlington," also included a tennis court. The property was sold after the children married and left home, and both refused to look at the site ever again after it was demolished to make way for flats.[9]

Southgate had been a relatively small community until the 1930s when development began in earnest, with the building of large homes, detached or semi-detached. The opening of an extension of the Piccadilly underground line to Southgate in 1933 further led to an increase in residents. Ted Ray is one of its most prominent residents, along with Sir Thomas Lipton, of tea fame, who lived there in the last years of his life.

However, Ted Ray's choice of Southgate was not because it was home to other celebrities, but rather it was in North London, and the comedian driving home from a gig outside of London in the North of England or the Midlands could feel he was closer to home as he approached the city from the North.

With the house, a car, a wife and eventually two sons, Ted Ray was very much an ordinary bloke, albeit a somewhat prosperous one. It might well argued that he epitomized the upper middle class, and his life was everything that members of his audience might yearn for.

As someone who named himself after a well-known golfer, it should be no surprise that Ted Ray was also an enthusiastic player; in later years he had an 8-handicap. He belonged to the Crews Hill Golf Club, founded in 1913 and with a course completed in 1922. In 1948, Ted Ray was elected captain of the Vaudeville Golfing Society, founded in 1921, and which he brought to play at the Club. Other members of the Society at the same time as Ted Ray were Jimmy Jewel and Ben Warriss, Donald Peers, Jerry Desmonde, and Sid Field. Despite being comedians, all were very serious about their golf. Also, at the Crews Hill Golf Club, he founded the OOTEGS (the One over the Eight Golfing Society), which had nine golfers present at its inaugural meeting. Another comedian member of the Club was Reg Varney, who painted in oil a landscape that dominated the clubhouse dining room.

In 1957, the comedian wrote an introduction to George Houghton's *The Truth about Golf Addicts: An Anthology of Carefree Notes and Drawings* (Museum Press), and in 1963, along with Bob Monkhouse, Arthur Askey, Ken Dodd, and others, he contributed to *Off the Tee: Favorite Golfing Stories and Anecdotes of the Famous* (W. Foulsham). In 1972, he published a volume of which he was the sole author, the anecdotal *Golf: My Slice of Life* (W.H. Allen), and that same Ted Ray contributed the foreword to *The Wit of Golf* (Leslie Frewin).

Obviously, it is more than coincidence that an entertainer who came to enjoy golf so much should have selected the name of a legendary golfer as his stage name. How early in his life Ted Ray became a golf enthusiast is not clear, but his knowledge of the Open Golf Championship at the time he selected the name of "Ted Ray" is indicative of an early interest in the sport. In later years, he joked, "Golf is a fascinating game. It has taken me forty years to discover that I can't play it."

1. Carroll Levis (1910-1968) was a Canadian-born entertainer who was heard on the BBC hosting a showcase for unknown performers. In later years he toured with the show titled *The Carroll Levis Discovery Show*, and it was also seen on television. Hughie Green's *Opportunity Knocks* was claimed to be a "rip-off" of the Carroll Levis show.

2. Stanelli was born Edward Stanelli de Groot (1895-1961) in Dublin, and both composed music and acted as well as playing the violin,

3. Figure skater Cecelia College (1920-2008) was a 1936 Olympic Silver Medalist, a 1937 World Champion and six times British National Champion.

4. "Soaring Salaries of British Vaude Acts Worry Bookers; Some Up 100%," p. 46.

5. Ted Ray, *Raising the Laughs*, p. 135.

6. Quoted in Lous Barfe, *Turned Out Nice Again: The Story of British Home Entertainment*, p. 74.

7. Broadcast on the BBC Light Programme, *Up the Pole* was heard from 1947 through 1952 and had the stars running an Arctic trading post.

8. Susan Ray recalls that sister Lena and a family friend, Glad, would also come by to socialize with Sybil and help her take care of the house.

9. Susan Ray e-mail to Anthony Slide, August 23, 2020.

CHAPTER FOUR

Radio and Ray's a Laugh

It is surprising that Ted Ray was adverse to being heard on radio in the 1930s and most of the 1940s. Although the reality is that he was so active on the music hall and variety stage that he really didn't have time for radio.

Music Hall

His radio debut came about thanks to producer John Sharman, a former music hall performer, famous for his cat act, who was producing a sixty-minute variety show titled *Music Hall*. On the staff of the BBC since the mid-1920s, John Sharman worked with the corporation's head of variety, John Watt, who once made the statement that "there are only six jokes in the world, and the I assure you that the BBC cannot broadcast three of them." *Music Hall* was heard every Saturday night, and was very much the broadcaster's star entertainment vehicle. *Music Hall* was first heard on March 26, 1932, and was the first BBC program to be presented in front of a live audience. The emphasis was very much on music hall, and topping that first bill was Gus Elen, the Coster Comedian whose famous songs included "If She Belonged to Me" and "If It Wasn't for the 'Ouses in Between." The former had Gus Elen threatening violence with a hammer as he sang what would happen to a friend's wife if she was married to him. Advocates of political correctness would cringe.

Music Hall continued to be produced by John Sharman until January 1949, when he retired, but the series itself continued until July 1952. An impressive run.

Ted Ray was heard on the show, whose stars also included the Western Brothers, in September 1939. It was broadcast from St. George's Hall, which also housed the BBC's new theatre organ, but which was destroyed in a March 1943 bombing raid. The comedian was quite pleased with his introduction to a new medium, but was horrified when the producer came to his dressing room after the show to tell him that while the live broadcast on the BBC Home Service was fine, there was a technical glitch in recording the show for the overseas market. Ted Ray had to repeat his entire act, without change and for the same audience.

Music Hall was followed by the first episode of *Just Fooling*, an hour-long variety entertainment which took its inspiration from George Black's "Crazy Gang" shows at the London Palladium. The star of the show was musical comedy star Binnie Hale, and the highspot was Joe O'Gorman, who began a performance of Harry Champion's music hall song, "Any Old Iron," only to have Champion himself interrupt and show him how it should be done. *Variety* (September 9, 1939) reported that Ted Ray's turn, "Fiddling and Fooling," consisted only of a short number, and offers no opinion as to the act.

Just Fooling was intended to be a new radio series, but its first broadcast was somewhat unfortunately on September 2nd, 1939. The previous day, Hitler had invaded Poland, and the following day, September 3rd, Britain and France declared war on Germany. There were no further episodes of *Just Fooling*.

At this time, certainly, Ted Ray did not become anything approaching a regular on the BBC. In May 1940, he and Cyril Fletcher were heard on the BBC's *Radio Party Night*. To avoid the threat of a Nazi bombing radio on the show's participants, the venue was not announced, but rather described as simply a "South Coast Hotel." That pretty much constitutes Ted Ray's wartime broadcasting career.

Ray's a Laugh

It is probably no exaggeration to claim that the radio series with which Ted Ray is most identified, *Ray's a Laugh*, came about thanks to the death of the star of another radio series. That star was Tommy Handley and the series was *ITMA*, an abbreviation of the phrase, *It's That Man Again*.[1] *ITMA* was a new type of radio series, reliant upon a series of ongoing characters, which first began broadcasting in July 1939, saw the nation through World War Two, and continued broadcasting for some twelve series until January 6, 1949.

Tommy Handley (1892-1949) was generally regarded as the greatest radio comedian of all time, and he was, needless to report, born in Liverpool. It would seem that every great radio comedian of this period –Tommy Handley, Arthur Askey and Ted Ray — was either born in Liverpool or grew up there. He had been something of a fixture on the BBC since the mid-1920s, and in the 1930s, he teamed up with Ronald Frankau, as already noted, performing as "Mr. Murgatroyd and Mr.

Winterbottom." When he died three days after what was to be the last *ITMA* show to be broadcast, the series died with him.

Even prior to the demise of *ITMA*, a BBC producer named George Inns had been trying to come up with a concept that would embrace the Ted Ray style of comedy. George Inns (1912-1970) had started his career at the BBC as a page boy at the age of fourteen. He had moved on to work in the sound effects department, and is credited with the sound effects for the first play to be broadcast by the BBC, *The Man with the Flower in His Hand*, on July 14th, 1930. It is also claimed that it is George Inns' voice that is heard shouting "In Town Tonight" in the introduction to the popular series of that title, first heard in 1930.

George Inns was anxious to prove his capability as a major radio producer, and he did so with three shows, *Forces Favorites, Jewel and Warriss Up the Pole* and *Ray's a Laugh*. He moved over to BBC Television in 1955, and three years later he created what is surely the corporation's most embarrassing and politically incorrect series, the weekly *The Black and White Minstrel Show*, with its singers, under the direction of George Mitchell, in blackface, which was seen on television from 1958 through 1976, which transferred to the stage at the Victoria Palace from 1962 through 1972, and for which George Inns was presented with the MBE (Member of the Most Excellent Order of the British Empire) by Queen Elizabeth in 1966.

At the time of George Inns' death, the managing director of the BBC, Huw Weldon said,

"The achievement of *The Black and White Minstrel Show*, which has remained fresh and, inventive and vigorous show after show for over 12 years, is a fitting memorial to a man who was in himself a complete television producer."

It was George Inns who gathered together the cast for *Ray's a Laugh* and suggested that the center piece should be a domestic scene. The title is credited to the comedian and to a friend and producer Sidney Smith, who conceived of it while driving home on Christmas Eve from a booking in Bristol.

According to the *Daily Herald* (January 27, 1949),

"The B.B.C. has decided that Ted — who broadcasts infrequently — is the only solo comic who is big enough in personality and versatility to take over where Tommy Handley left off.

"Michael Standing, the B.B.C.'s head of variety,[2] has approached Ted with the offer, and Ted has accepted. The first programme of the weekly series goes on in April. It may occupy the Thursday night 'live' spot on the Home Service, before repeat transmissions on the Light — the old *ITMA* times.

"Name of the programme? It hasn't been decided yet. In may be *My Good Friends* or *MGF*."

Ted Ray told the *Daily Herald*, "The idea is that we shall have a weekly funny family affair. I shall compere, do some dialogue, and my own comic act." In reality, it was a little more than that, although it is obvious from the comedian's comment, not to mention the ultimate title, that this was very much one man's show.

The script was the work of E.A. (Eddie) Maguire and George Wadmore. The latter came up with the gags, while Eddie Maguire handled the domestic sequences, with Ted Ray himself suggesting situations that had developed in his own household. Eddie Maguire went on to write for television, credited with episodes of *Coronation Street* and *Dr. Finlay's Casebook*. George Wadmore (1923-1988) also worked in television, writing for comedian Charlie Drake on *Drake's Progress* and for *The Ted Ray Show*. (According to the usually reliable Denis Gifford, the first episode of *Ray's a Laugh* was written by George Wadmore and Ronnie Hanbury, who also wrote *Life with the Lyons*.[3]) Ted Ray contributed to the scripts, and later episodes are credited to Sid Colin, Talbot Rothwell, Charles Hart, and Bernard Botting.

Con Mahoney, who was later head of BBC radio light entertainment, recalled,

"The writing started on a Monday evening and it was my first sight of a genuine team operation. The session began at around 6 p.m. and a rota dispatched one of the team to the Grosvenor Arms [the local pub] for the necessary lubricants — invariably champagne. Ted dominated and gave everybody the main structures on which the funnies would be woven, although George Wadmore was rightfully recognized as the gag man supreme. Eddie Maguire, who became the regular writer of the domestic spot, was outstandingly skilled at giving the right measure to the lovable tiffs between Kitty and "Mr. Ray" — a form of address Kitty always used when off-stage."[4]

Barry Took wrote, "Story lines were crisp and direct, the jokes funny, the characters well-rounded if not over subtle. It was very much Ted Ray's show."[5]

Ray's a Laugh embraced a relatively simple format, and really had nothing new to offer in terms of originality in content, beginning with the radio equivalent of a stand-up comedy routine (with the opening words, "Well, boys and girls"), followed by a domestic scene, in which Ted Ray was a private detective with the Cannon Enquiry Agency and later a reporter on the *Daily Bugle,* and concluding with "George, the Man with the Conscience." The opening signature tune was somewhat simplistic:

"Ray's a Laugh! Ray's a Laugh!
"When You're Feeling Sad and Blue just
"Raise a Laugh!"

Ted Ray contributed the closing song, "My Friends and I Are Saying Goodbye Now." The closing song may initially have been written when the show was tentatively titled *My Good Friends.*

As the comedian recalled, "My fiddling and fooling on the stage had to be changed to new methods for the mike…Yet after I reached home from the first number of *Ray's a Laugh* my wife greeted me with a shake of the head…Before number two of the series went on the air the show was re-shaped."[6]

The first seven series were broadcast on the BBC Home Service, with the final five series broadcast on the Light Programme. The first show was pre-recorded, but all subsequent shows were broadcast live from the Paris Cinema on Lower Regent Street. Initially, the show, every episode of which was thirty minutes in length, was heard on Monday nights, then Tuesday nights. As of series two, it was aired on Thursday evenings, until series nine when it moved to Friday evenings. There were some special shows on different nights: *Ted and Kitty's Christmas* was broadcast on Monday, December 25th, 1950, *Ted and Kitty's Easter Outing* was broadcast on Monday, April 6th, 1953, and series six was retitled *Ted Ray's Time* and broadcast on Monday evenings from October 1954 through April 1955. That final season featured Jewish comedian Harold Berens, who introduced two female characterizations, Mrs. Twiddleswitch and Mrs. Mosseltoff.

Ted Ray had to adapt for the new medium. As he explained,

"This method of coming to terms with my [theater] audience is lost to me on the air, and so are attitudes and facial expressions. In my broadcasts I find substitutes for these in dialects and characters into which I can enter and build up a picture in the listener's mind. I greatly enjoy my stage work and the close contact with a living and responsive audience, but the creative demand of radio presentation appeals to me, too. Each week the programme must be there, different and original for the benefit of the most porous thing in the world — the microphone. It is all very stimulating."[7]

From the beginning, it was agreed that the high spot of the show was the domestic spot. Playing opposite Ted Ray as his wife was Australian Kitty Bluett.

Kitty Bluett (1916-1994) was actually born in the Brixton area of London, the daughter of a small-time comedian, and her sister, Belle, was married to Jimmy Jewel, who pops up so often in the Ted Ray story. At the age of ten, she was taken by her parents to Australia, where she was partnered on radio with Dick Bentley, who was to become one of the stars of *Take It from Here* with Jimmy Edwards. In Australia, she was featured in a couple of very minor films, *A Tank in Australia* (1942), written and directed by Alf Goulding (who also played a Japanese spy), and *A Son Is Born* (1948), directed by Eric Porter, in which she played opposite three future international leading men, Ron Randall, Peter Finch and John McCallum. (Kitty at one time planned to marry Ron Randall.)

Returning to the U.K., Kitty Bluett made one film there, *What a Carry On!* (1949), directed by John E. Blakeley, and starring Jimmy Jewel, Ben Warriss and Joseph Locke. The film has no connection to the later "Carry On" series.

As early as the summer of 1949, Kitty Bluett and Ted Ray took to the stage, promoting their radio show, at the Stoll Theatre, London, on July 15th. Radio listeners, it was reported, actually believed that Ted Ray and Kitty Bluett were a married couple. In case audiences at the recordings should think similarly, Mrs. Ted Ray was always to be found there, seated in the front row.

The radio partnership came to an end in July 1954, when the BBC announced that it was to end the radio marriage of Ted Ray and Kitty Bluett. The thousands of listeners who thought the couple married, now had to deal with a divorce engineered by the BBC. Changes were needed to the format. After finishing his summer season at Great Yarmouth, Ted Ray returned to London for a new series. "It will be an all-new show," explained the BBC, "But we haven't worked out the details yet."[8]

Beginning October 13th, 1955, for one season, Diane Hart became Ted Ray's new radio wife, Mary, and Kenneth Connor took on the role of his brother-in-law, Harold. He also had a new boss, played by Alexander Gauge. Diane Hart (1926-2002) was a RADA trained actress, who had worked on the variety stage as double act with Pat Aza. Plump Alexander Gauge (1914-1960) is probably best known for playing Friar Tuck on the television series, *The Adventures of Robin Hood* from 1955 through 1959.

Perhaps Kitty Bluett had a premonition that her time on the show was about to come to an end when in April 1954, she took to the stage of the

Metropolitan, Edgware Road, with an act consisting of stories about her husband. Once she was done with the show, the stories might certainly become more interesting for music hall audiences. In fact, Kitty Bluett was no newcomer to the music hall stage, having sung and told stories in April 1950 at the Wood Green Empire and the Walthamstow Palace.

There are those who are positively savage in their criticism of Kitty Bluett, complaining of her rasping voice, and suggested that the number of times she and Ted Ray refer to each other as "darling" made it sound rather like a dirty word. He describes her mother as "the Gestapo in bloomers," and notes that "We trust each other like Truman and Stalin." Certainly, Kitty Bluett's adenoidal delivery of lines is far from attractive, and her choice as Ted Ray's radio wife is hard to comprehend from a modern perspective.

One wonders if the BBC had a penchant for Australian actresses, with Joy Nichols co-starring on *Take It from Here* almost simultaneous with Kitty Bluett on *Ray's a Laugh*. What did these antipodean leading ladies have that a good English actress did not?

Kitty Bluett's career was pretty much over after she was let go from the show. On December 17th, 1955, at the Marylebone Registry Office, she married producer Julian Jover, and moved back to Australia with him, but the couple divorced in 1980. It was her second marriage.

Aside from Kitty Bluett, the most important cast member at the beginning of the series was probably Fred Yule (1893-1982), a well-known character comedian who had introduced the characters of Bigga Banga and Norman the Doorman on *ITMA*. A music hall comedian, he had actually appeared in an early television production of *The Beggar's Opera* for the BBC in 1937. He joined *ITMA* in the early 1940s, playing Tommy Handley's brother-in-law. His popularity on *ITMA* made Fred Yule a natural casting choice for *Ray's a Laugh*, on which he played Kitty's brother, Nelson with his high-pitched voice.

And then, there is the most famous of cast members on the show, and that is Peter Sellers, who is heard in the first six series. While performing on *Ray's a Laugh*, Peter Sellers was also being heard from 1951 through 1960 on *The Goon Show*, a BBC series that today has taken on legendary and cult status, unlike, sadly, Ted Ray's first major venture into radio.

Peter Sellers was heard in the domestic episodes on *Ray's a Laugh*, and his characters with their individual catchphrases are still remembered if not with affection certainly with a certain comic delight. There is the neighbor from across the street, Crystal Jollibottom, whose catchphrases include "I'll thank you to stop fiddling with my feather duster,"

"Me unmentionables are caught round me scrubbing brush," and "You old saucebox." Soppy, the boy, tells everyone to "shut up, big gob." Two Italian characters are Luigi and Giuseppi, with the former asking, "What you a-want, supposing we a-got it?" Another ethnic characterization was Serge Suit, a friendly Russian, who would announce, "I lerewike to hear Tchaikerowovsky's Serewugar Plerewum Ferwairy." Wilberforce is a detective, assuring, "Hist, never fear, Hugo's here." And scout leader, Cedric, pointing out, "Life gets humdrum if you don't dabble."

As evidence of recognition of Peter Seller's contribution to the show, his initial fee of nine guineas per episode was raised to twenty-five guineas, the same amount as Kitty Bluett received. Ted Ray's salary was 105 pounds per show.

Peter Sellers spoke in admiration of Ted Ray, whom he credited with teaching him much about acting and timing. His family and the Ray family actually went on vacation together to Pevensey Bay on the South Coast.

Rounding out the cast of players on *Ray's a Laugh* are familiar names from British comedy: Patricia Hayes (in the first five series), Kenneth Connor (in series five through twelve, playing odd job man, Herbert Toil, and others), with Graham Stark ("If you haven't been to Manchester, you haven't lived"), Charles Leno (as "Dear Old Dad" who "lost all his faith in human nature"), Laidman Brown (who was Ted Ray's new boss, Mr. Trumble), and Pat Coombs (who joined the show in September 1961). Percy Edwards provided animal impersonations, for which he was famed,[9] George, the Man with the Conscience, was played by Leslie Perrins, a very well-spoken actor not usually associated with comedy.

Patricia Hayes had been active on radio since 1922. She had been heard on the Max Wall vehicle, *Our Shed*, and from there, she moved on to *Ray's a Laugh*. As she recalled, she needed the work badly because her marriage had come to an end and she had three children to support. "During the five-and-a-half years I worked with Ted, I was never out of the house for more than half a day a week. That was how long it took to rehearse and record a radio show, but the repeat fees turned that one half day's work into a respectable income."[10]

Musical interludes were provided by Stanley Black and His Dance Orchestra. A musical group, sounding very pseudo-American, the Beaux and the Belles, was put together by singer Johnny Johnson, who had sung duets with Kathryn Grayson as part of her act at the London Palladium, with Ted Ray also on the bill. Ted Ray and Kitty Bluett also recorded three numbers together in 1951: "Count on Me" and "Dearie" (Columbia, D.B. 2698), "Let's Put Out the Lights" and "An Ordinary

Broom" (Columbia, D.B. 2760) and "Easy Come, Easy Go" and "Cute Little Hat" (Columbia, D.B. 2921).

("Dearie," written by Bob Hilliard and Dave Mann has been recorded by an eclectic group of performers, including the Five Smith Bros. [on Parlophone Records]Tessie O'Shea and Nat Jackley in reference to their appearance in *Out of This World* at the New Opera House, Blackpool, in 1950, and, of all people, Richard Attenborough.)

"We bring you melody from out of the sky, my brother and I." What fond memories those lyrics evoked at one time of the close harmony singing duo, Bob and Alf Pearson, with Bob at the piano. The brothers were supposedly the first double act to be seen on BBC Television in the 1930s. Multi-talented Bob also acted on the show, playing the role of Jennifer, who was usually introduced with Ted Ray's saying, "Why, it's a little girl, what's your name?" The answer was always, "Jennnniifffffeeeerrrr!" Another characterization from Bob was that of Mrs. Hoskin — with the catchphase, "Ooh, it's agony, Ivy" — and with the aforementioned Ivy played by Ted Ray.

Bob and Alf Pearson made their final appearance on *Ray's a Laugh* in July 1951. They were replaced by John Hanson, who certainly couldn't handle comedy routines, but was well known to audiences for his endless touring productions of such classic musical comedies as *The Desert Song* and *The Student Prince*. On *The Betty Witherspoon Show*, there is a joke about the worst punishment in the French Foreign Legion, which is touring in *The Desert Song* with John Hanson.

Radio comedy does not lend itself to the printed page. Written down, it might at best seem good-humored, but generally it has nothing else to offer the reader. Dialogue from *Ray's a Laugh* has not stood the test of time. However, it would be wrong not to include some sampling of the Ted Ray/ Kitty Bluett routines from the show:

TED: Now what have you got for lunch?

KITTY: Egg and chips.

TED: Eggs again. I've had so many eggs in the last month, every time I walk down the gravel path I scratch!

KITTY: Ted! Anyway, do you know what you've got for a sweet?

TED *(adopting a Charles Boyer accent):* You — my darling — Kitty from the Casbah — give me a kiss…

KITTY: I've got some French pastry for you.

TED: You are my French pastry! Come here!

KITTY: Stop it, Ted! I've made you a sponge cake, with jelly, cream and a cherry on top.

TED: I am not a man to be trifled with. Come…geev me a kiss.

KITTY: Ted — behave yourself!

TED: Well, you've never kissed me between the sink and the cellar steps.

KITTY: Go away, you silly thing! Flirting in the kitchen! I thought you were past that sort of thing.

TED: Listen — just because there's frost on the windows, it doesn't mean that the boiler's gone out.

Not only incredibly unfunny, but also rehashing some very old gags, as in the last line. What must seem most unlikely to anyone today is that the domestic sequences would resonate with listeners, recalling similar events and marital conversations in their own lives. Yet, as the *Daily Herald* (May 5, 1950) pointed out, "Consistently and concisely it is true-to-life domesticity, mirroring brutally and funnily every husband and wife in the country."

Supposedly the BBC understood what working classes audiences wanted, and used *Ray's a Laugh* to bring their lives to radio. In that working class life, particularly at this time, was somewhat miserable, it seems unlikely that members of that group would have any wish in listening to what BBC executives considered to be an insight into their lives.

Ray's a Laugh was last heard on January 13th, 1961, played off with the closing theme song, "You Are My Sunshine." The name lived on thanks to a race horse being named "Ray's a Laugh."

Calling All Forces

Ted Ray may have been a busy man in the 1930s and 1940s with stage appearances, and he was equally busy on radio in the following decade, Not only was he heard on *Ray's a Laugh*, but he also hosted *Calling All Forces* which was heard on the BBC Light Programme and on the BBC Overseas Service for troops in Korea and Malaya. It was first broadcast on Sunday, December 3rd, 1950, with Petula Clark, dubbed as the Forces Sweetheart or Singing Sweetheart, and Leslie Welch, billed as the Memory Man. Ted Ray was the original star, on air every week, through April 7th, 1952, when Charlie Chester and Tony Hancock took over.

"All this was a very long time ago," writes Petula Clark. "Though I remember Ted with affection…He was a lovely man, and very talented too."[11]

Petula Clark appears to have left the show at the same time as Ted Ray. She had been introduced each week with the chorus of "Let Me Call You Sweetheart, and the audience was informed she brought greetings and sang the most requested songs. The show was scripted by Bob Monkhouse and Denis Goodwin. Petula Clark would sing songs of the servicemen's choice. Leslie Welch (1907-1980) had an act which consisted of nothing more than his answering any question the audience might have, proving that he had a perfect memory for facts. *Calling All Forces* also had a catchphrase used by Ted Ray, "You should have used stronger elastic!"

There were other radio broadcasts concurrent with *Ray's a Laugh*. From October 1957 through March 1958, Ted Ray hosted the long-running sixty-minute, radio version of a music hall bill, *Variety Playhouse*, heard on the BBC Home Service beginning in May 1953. From October 1956 through April 1957, Jack Hulbert and Cicely Courtneidge co-starred with an ongoing sketch titled "Pocket Theatre." Also on the Home Service, he could be heard starring in *The Spice of Life*, "a carefree mixture of comedy and music," which ran an awkward forty-five minutes for some twenty-six weeks, beginning October 8th, 1956. June Whitfield recalled,

"I popped up as various debs, tarts and old bats, but my main spot was a regular double act with Ted, in which we played two wrinkly old girls in a laundrette, Mrs. Pinny (Ted) and Mrs. Drool (me)…We swapped stories about our aches and pains and hopeless husbands, with a good measure of 'Ooooh yeeeees, Mrs. Drool. Ooooh, Mrs. Pinny, I knowww.'

"*The Spice of Life* hardly registered with the public, but it did nothing to dent Ted's tremendous popularity. I think he was reckoned to be the highest-paid comic in the country at one time."[12]

With the demise of *Ray's a Laugh*, Ted Ray didn't take any time off from radio. He starred in a couple of sketch shows: *Once Over Lightly*, with Dick Bentley, as proprietors of a weekly newspaper, *Weekly Once Over*, a series of fifteen, thirty-minute programs, broadcast on the BBC Light Programme from October 1961 through January 1962; and *Ted*

Ray and the..., with Paul Whitsun-Jones, a series of twelve, thirty-minute programs, broadcast on the BBC Light Programme from October through December 1962. The first episode was titled *Ted Ray and the Tuba*, the second *Ted Ray and the Elephant*, and so on. There were also a couple of one-offs, *Let Bye-Laws Be Bye-Laws*, with Charlie Chester, a thirty-minute show on the BBC Light Programme, May 9th, 1963; and *Ted Ray Says Be My Guest*, a thirty-minute show on Radio 2, broadcast on December 3rd, 1968.

Let Bye-Laws Be Bye-Laws was one show from a series titled *Star Parade*, and also emanating from *Star Parade* was the sitcom, *How's Your Father?*, which was first heard as what might considered a pilot episode on September 22nd, 1963. It returned as a series of nine thirty-minute episodes on the BBC Light Programme from April 10th through June 5th, 1964.

Written by Denis Goodwin, *How's Your Father?* featured Thora Hird as Ted Ray's housekeeper, Mrs. Bender, Eleanor Summerfield as his sister Ethel, Annette André as Angela Bender, and real-life son, Robin Ray, as radio son Robin Ray. Pat Coombs and Terence Alexander were also regular members of the cast. Despite a good cast, the sitcom generated no interest from the critics and little interest from listeners.

("How's Your Father?" is a British slang expression, somewhat difficult to explain in polite terms. Basically, if one is asked if one want a bit of How's Your Father, it would be an invitation to sexual intercourse.)

Does the Team Think?

Ted Ray ended his radio career with the series with which today he is most associated, and that is the panel game *Does the Team Think?* It is not the first panel game with which the comedian was associated. For a short time, a mere eleven episodes heard on the BBC Light Programme from October through December 1955, he had been on *My Wildest Dream*, along with Tommy Trinder and Jimmy Edwards, with both of whom he was reunited on *Does the Team Think?* Harry Secombe was also a member of the panel, which was kept in check (almost) by chairman Peter Haigh. The concept was for panel members to uncover secret ambitions of members of the studio audience.

The Sketch (October 19, 1955) pointed out to its readers that between them, Ted Ray, Tommy Trinder, Jimmy Edwards, and Harry Secombe earned 100,000 pounds a year. One suspects that Tommy Trinder was the highest paid, followed by Ted Ray.

Does the Team Think? was the brainchild of Jimmy Edwards, the highly successful star of radio's *Take It from Here*. The impetus was the BBC radio program, *Any Questions*, hosted by Freddie Griswood, which began in 1948, and which consisted of celebrities answering questions of topical interest. The only proviso was that none of the questions could relate to anything that might be debated in the next two weeks in the Houses of Parliament.

The whole concept was obviously ripe for parody, and the result was *Does the Team Think?*, on which comedians would answer questions from the audience with the emphasis on laughter evoked through one-liners, impromptu gags and the like.

The BBC brought Peter Haigh from Granada Television's panel show *My Wildest Dream* as the host of the program, and the first episode was aired on the Light Programme on October 6th, 1957. Actor David Tomlinson was the only panelist in every episode of the first season, which ran through December 22nd. On the first three, he was joined by comedian Jimmy Wheeler and magician David Nixon. Jimmy Wheeler was on all but one of the episodes, when he was replaced by comedian Alfred Marks, but the third guest might be George Martin (best known for his work with the Beatles), Jon Pertwee (the third Dr. Who), or Arthur English (well known to American audiences for his appearances on *Are You Being Served?*).

Changes were made for the second season, which was first aired on June 1st, 1958. McDonald Hobley, a popular BBC announcer, took over as host. Tommy Trinder, harmonica player Larry Adler and Arthur Askey were the new regulars for the first three programs, and on the fourth (airing on June 22nd, 1958), Ted Ray became a regular panelist. His presence enhanced the show, assuring its long-term success, and he was to remain a regular panelist basically for the entire run through July 19th, 1976. Tommy Trinder and Arthur Askey were his most frequent co-panelists, but he also might be joined by Cyril Fletcher, Bernard Braden, and Richard Murdoch. Robin Ray was invited to participate on October 13th, 1970. The emphasis was obviously on male comedians, but there were a few women on the show through the years, including Beryl Reid, Barbara Kelly (who was married to Bernard Braden), Catherine (Katie) Boyle, Jean Kent, Nancy Spain, Joan Sims, June Whitfield, and Joan Turner. Even Jessie Matthews and Barbara Cartland made it on the show, but none might be considered a regular.

Cyril Fletcher recalled that "Ted Ray was the kingpin and was very, very quick indeed. He had a computer mind which dredged up the exactly right old tried and true jokes required for the immediate moment, and allied to this he had a rapier-like wit and speed of delivery which enabled him to come out with original witticisms as well."[13]

There was a total of twenty-one seasons of the show. There was also a BBC television version, with Ted Ray, Jimmy Edwards, Bernard Braden, and various guest panelists, which was broadcast from May 28th through August 13th, 1961. Thames Television broadcast two seasons in 1982 and 1983, without Ted Ray, but with Beryl Reid and Frankie Howerd. *Does the Team Think?* was revived for two series on BBC Radio 2 in 2007 and 2009, hosted by Vic Reeves. It was not a success.

Does the Team Think? continued on its merry way, proving that Ted Ray was arguably the most quick-witted comedian in the U.K. Aside from the panel game, the comedian's radio career ended, to all extents and purposes, in 1973 with *The Betty Witherspoon Show*, which is forgotten today but which is a magnificent ending to a radio career and a show deserving of much wider recognition.

In 1968, Ted Ray and Kenneth Williams had appeared on television being interviewed by David Frost on *Frost on Sunday*, and given full reign to show off their comic genius. There was a strike on at the time and the two men had to cross a picket line; it says something for their politics that neither found this more than a minor inconvenience. The couple had also worked together on *Carry On Teacher*. And it is very obvious from their appearances together and their public comments that they admired each other, they enjoyed each other's company and they could laugh at each other's humor. "You could never fail, Ken, because you listen to people," Ted Ray told his colleague, who acknowledged, "Coming from a performer of his stature I was greatly touched and complimented."[14]

So close were the two men that Ted Ray's wife, Sybil, would go on holiday with Kenneth Williams' mother, Louie. Kenneth Williams is also godfather to Andrew's son, Mark.

At the end of his career, Ted Ray was featured in more than twenty episodes of the BBC Children's Television series, *Jackanory*, from 1966 through 1975. In September and October, 1970, the comedian narrated the classic children's story of "Thomas the Tank Engine" in five parts, adapted by Howard Kennett: "The Three Railway Engines," "Thomas the Tank Engine," "Duck and the Diesel Engine," "Toby the Train Engine," and "The Eight Famous Engines." In the same series was Kenneth Williams, appearing in more than sixty programs in which celebrities read books for children, adding mannerisms and voice characterizations of their own.

The Betty Witherspoon Show

It has been suggested that the BBC decided to produce *The Betty Witherspoon Show* because it felt the need for a comedy series that would make good use of the talents of two radio comedians without ongoing series. *Ray's a Laugh* had, of course, ended it run. Kenneth Williams had been a leading player, along with star Kenneth Horne on *Around the Horne*, but it was cancelled when Kenneth Horne died in 1969, and the "successor" *Stop Messing About*, with Kenneth Williams, ran for only two seasons.

BBC producer David Hatch had signed Kenneth Williams for *Just a Minute*, a radio program on which panelists spoke for one minute on any given subject. He was a regular on the show from 1968 until his death in 1988. In the summer of 1972, Hatch and Williams discussed an idea for a revue-type radio show, and the result was *The Betty Witherspoon Show*, which would present Ted Ray and Kenneth Williams with equal billing. Simon Brett, who went on to a successful career as a writer of mystery novels, produced (although the pilot episode was produced by David Hatch). Music was provided by pianist Neil Innes, together with Ted Ray deliberately playing not too well on the violin, with help from recorded music and a host of special sound effects.[15] The comedian explained that the BBC had been flooded with letters — "not a flood more a drip really" — asking that he perform on the violin, which he does, despite continued interruptions from Kenneth Williams. The two main scriptwriters were Michael Wale and Joe Steeples, with additional material from a variety of writers, the best known of which was David Nobbs. Both Wale and Steeples have been described as excellent journalists who knew nothing about writing comedy.

A pilot show was recorded on Sunday June 25th, 1972, at the Playhouse Theatre. The series was picked up for a further ten episodes, and they were recorded, between October 1972 and January 1973 on Monday mornings at the Paris Cinema on Lower Regent Street, first at lunch time and then at 10:30 a.m. There was an immediate problem for the performers in that comedy doesn't necessarily work well on a Monday morning. The company received their scripts on the Sunday and rehearsals would take place on the Monday prior to recording. Audiences were not overly enthusiastic and the show was often recorded in front of a very small number. Actor Nigel Rees describes it as "an audience of deaf-mutes, all six of them." Listening to the entire series, it is sadly obvious that there are few people in the audience and towards the end the clapping and laughter barely registers. Only the last episode in the series drew a full house to the Paris

Cinema, with even Kenneth Williams' mother in the audience. As he wrote in his autobiography,

"It became a tedious chore and the scripts started taking a lot of the blame. By the 27th of November the producer told us that the BBC was trying to find new writers…I noted in my diary, 'The people who are the quickest to fault comic endeavours are invariably unfunny themselves.'"[16]

Despite being recorded in 1972 and early in 1973, the last one on January 22nd, the series was not broadcast until more than a year later, on Saturday evenings on Radio 2 from April 22nd through June 22nd, 1974. In total, apparently, some thirteen shows were actually recorded, but only ten shows broadcast with material from the other three shows integrated into those ten. Material from the pilot was also repeated in one of the later episodes.

Happily, all ten shows have survived, and they prove to be a delight to listen to. They are not as disappointing has been suggested. The humor is still, on the whole, funny, and at times the series achieves a surreal quality. Critics have written that the series required Ted Ray to act as a stooge to Kenneth Williams, but this is not true in that both comedians are equal in stature and neither is forced to be a straight man to the other. It is difficult to accept comments from critics of the show that Ted Ray objected to being a straight man, demanded script changes and diminished Kenneth Williams participation. Ted Ray and Kenneth Williams play well off one another, with what seems to be a certain amount of ad-libbing by the former, while Kenneth Williams lets it be known that much of the material is beneath his dignity. "We'd never have had this problem if we'd booked Yehudi Menuhin," he laments as Ted Ray picks up his violin. "Isn't it about time you retired?" asks Williams. There is quite a hint of gay humor, and Ted Ray seems to enjoy it as much as Kenneth Williams. The latter appears in each episode as Inspector Spewles of New Scotland Yard, who is given to calling Ted Ray "Sweetie." Despite all the gay innuendo, Kenneth Williams can still insist that we "keep it clean."

Jokes are still relatively funny, although some might argue they are rather dated:

TED: What's worn under the kilt?

MIRIAM: Nothing. Everything's in working order.

The initial joke, of course, is that this is *The Betty Witherspoon Show*, but she is not present, and, when introduced, is heard, following the theme song, "Happy Days Are Here Again," in the person of Ted Ray.

Supporting the stars is the brilliant Miriam Margolyes, still going strong, playing the character, "Mrs. Raquel Welch of Hendon," in each episode and usually sporting a Jewish or Scottish accent.[17] Even back then, she insisted on telling everyone she was a lesbian and farting incessantly. Ted Ray described her as looking like an "unmade bed." Miriam Margolyes is kinder in her remembrance of Ted Ray, describing him as "a lovely man. Funny, kind, competent."[18] She points out, "Truthfully I remember very little [about the show]. It was very much at the beginning of my career. Ted Ray was incredibly nice, a very relaxed personality, a lovely, warm, funny man, very well behaved."[19]

The fourth member of the company is Nigel Rees, at the start of his professional career, who provides a variety of voices and went on to devise and host the long-running (since 1976) radio show, *Quote…Unquote*, and to author more than fifty books.

He recalls in his diary that at the pilot recording, "Ted Ray arrived smelling of booze and very pink in the face but was remarkably sharp and fit…Miriam didn't feel too happy about the rather difficult atmosphere of 'us and them' but I was thrilled to bits to have an audience responding to my lines."

As of January 8th, he notes, "KW [Kenneth Williams] crept up to me and asked confidentially, 'Getting lots of fucks then, are you?' When I assented modestly, he nodded knowingly and said, 'That's what I've heard.'"[20]

Sadly, Nigel Rees does not share my enthusiasm for the show, writing, "Most of us were not at all impressed by the BW show. I have all of the recordings…but usually I find them pretty unbearable…I don't think the BBC was deliberately trying to ruin the show but shall we say, they didn't exactly go out of their way to help.

"I don't think it was a dispute over billing but Ted did feel that he wasn't given the right sort of prominence in the show (as you say I don't think he had any grounds for complaint). All I would add is that in his other work, Ted had a very, very sharp mind. He could whistle up a joke from his memory bank on any subject you threw at him."[21]

If the show itself seems surreal, there was an equally surreal quality to what was happening away from the microphone. Nigel Rees noted in his diary that Ted Ray "smells at times like a rather nasty accident in a lavatory."[22] Both Kenneth Williams and Ted Ray would go on about lavatories. "It's an obsession with Ted. He says he goes and sits on the loo every morning whether he needs to or not because he was once told this kept you regular. Then they both take sleeping tablets. Ted says he's always tossing and turning in the night, ideas going through his head. Miriam [Margolyes] said, in her Queenly voice, 'Oh, I just have a wank, that sends me off.'"[23] Miriam Margolyes, in fact, would say anything that came into her head without regard to the response or feelings of the individual to whom she was talking. At the last recording, on December 4th, Nigel Rees writes, "Despite some Mongol children in the audience, it went rather well this week because there were some lads on the front row who found everything hilarious."[24]

Each episode features a comic song, such as "The Type of Horrible Cockney Song That Killed the Music Hall" (episode one) and "Why Don't They Write Songs about Runcorn?" (episode three). Concluding each show was an episode from the "Theatre of the Air" (in series order): "A Tale of Two Cities," "Hound of the Baskervilles," "Russia — The Last Days of the Tsar," "Henry VIII," "Romeo and Juliet," "Wuthering Heights," "Anthony and Cleopatra," "The Permissive Society," "Nelson and Lady Hamilton," and "Join the Procrastinators Club" (actually a Foreign Legion drama).

Helena

Surprisingly, both in terms of casting and Ted Ray's obvious enthusiasm and respect for the production, for him one of the most important of his radio productions was not a comedy but a serious drama. Three pages of his autobiography are devoted to *Helena*, a play based on the 1950 novel by Evelyn Waugh, in which the comedian played the Wandering Jew.

Unfortunately, little information survives relating to the production, and Ted Ray's autobiography which is notably short in terms of dates does not provide even a year for its broadcast. The play was aired on BBC's Third Programme, which was devoted to serious works and classical music and which changed its name in 1967 to Radio 3. Delightfully, the BBC described the Third Programme as intended not to be educational but for the educated. The producer was the aristocratic Christopher Sykes, who had apparently been a big fan of *Ray's a Laugh*. He was also a close friend of Evelyn Waugh and had been a BBC radio producer since 1945.

In all probability, the play was broadcast in late 1951; the adaptation was reported to be in progress in October of that year. The title character is the mother of Constantine the Great who supposedly, among other things, discovered the true cross of Jesus. The cast was an impressive one, including John Gielgud, Flora Robson, Isabel Jeans, and Adelaide Hall. Despite the seriousness of the drama, Ted Ray's part was a comic one. When told by Helena that he must be old, he responds, "I'll say I am…I'm in incense, see…All the leading shrines are on my books…Why it's all on account of the Galiean that I'm here today."

The character of the Wandering Jew has popped up many times on screen, in plays and in novels, but never surely as a comic character such as this, played by the country's leading comedian.

Desert Island Discs

A look at Ted Ray's radio career would not be complete without reference to his participation in the long-running BBC series hosted by Roy Plomley, *Desert Island Discs*, on which celebrities select the recordings that they would like to have with them if stranded on a desert island. Ted Ray selects an eclectic group of recordings, a mix of serious and popular, and including one of his own. As a luxury item to take with him, Ted Ray selected hairnets.

On the classical side are Yehudi Menuhin playing Nicolò Paganini's "Romance" in A Minor (interesting in that there had been many jokes through the years in which the comedian had been compared, unfavorably, to the classical violinist); Sergei Rachmaninov playing Chopin's Waltz in E Minor; and Sir Thomas Beecham conducting the London Philharmonic Orchestra playing Tchaikovsky's Symphony No. 5 in E Minor.

On the popular side are Bob Hope and Shirley Ross singing "Thanks for the Memory" from *The Big Broadcast of 1938*, "Trumpet Rhapsody" played by Harry James, and Bing Crosby and Louis Armstrong performing "Gone Fishin'" (written in 1950 by Nick and Charles Kenny). He also selected the Columbia recording (D.B. 2774) of himself performing "Jack and the Giant Killer" with his son, Andrew, with music by Philip Green. (Not selected, but on the reverse side is "When Daddy Was a Boy.")

Should anyone consider it somewhat egocentric of Ted Ray to choose one of his own recordings, he or she should be reminded that when opera singer Elizabeth Schwarkopf was on *Desert Island Discs* she chose eight of her own recordings.

Andrew Ray never made it to *Desert Island Discs*, but his brother, Robin, did — on November 16th, 1964. His choice was somewhat more classical than that of his father:

The King's College Chapel (Cambridge) Choir singing "Once in Royal David's City"; Maurice Ravel's Piano Concerto for Left Hand in D Minor; Sergei Rachmaninov's Symphony No. 2 in E Minor; Giacomo

Puccini's "Piece en Forme de Habanera" and Chopin's Ballade No. 4 in F. Minor; playwright Alan Bennett Performing his monologue "Take a Pew" from *Beyond the Fringe*, and José Feliciano singing "Miss Otis Regrets".

1. "It's that Man Again" was a phrase used at the time to refer to Hitler.

2. Michael Standing (1910-1984) was actually the BBC's controller of entertainment, the son of actor Sir Guy Standing and the brother of actress Kay Hammond.

3. Denis Gifford, *The Golden Age of Radio*, p. 239.

4. Con Mahoney, "Ted Ray," *The Stage*, November 17, 1977, p. 15.

5. Barry Took, *Laughter in the Air*, p. 93.

6. "Steam Radio…I Love It Says Ted Ray."

7. "Ted Ray Tells the Difference," p. 3.

8. The *Daily Mirror*, July 5, 1954, p. 6.

9. Percy Edwards (1908-1966) came to fame largely thanks to *Ray's a Laugh*. It is claimed he could impersonate 600 birds and assorted animals, for which (incredibly) he was made a member of the Order of the British Empire (MBE) in 1993.

10. Quoted in Barry Took, *Laughter in the Air*, p. 94.

11. Petula Clark, e-mail to Anthony Slide, September 5, 2020.

12. June Whitfield, *…and June Whitfield*, p. 125.

13. Cyril Fletcher, *Nice One Cyril*, p. 91.

14. Kenneth Williams, *Just Williams: An Autobiography*, p. 226.

15. In "Steam Radio…I Love It Says Ted Ray," he writes of radio having its stars in the Sound Effects Department: "They give us armies fighting–boats rippling along a river- a comedian flying out through the roof. Oh yes, and that spring in my bed."

16. Ibid, p. 283.

17. The actress' father was born on the South Side of Glasgow, and to this day, she can still speak with a perfect Scottish, or as she would claim, Glasgow accent.

18. Miriam Margolyes, e-mail to Anthony Slide, September 3, 2020.

19. Anthony Slide interview with Miriam Margolyes, September 5, 2020.

20. Nigel Rees, *My Radio Times*.

21. Nigel Rees, e-mail to Anthony Slide, August 9, 2020.

22. Diary entry dated October 23rd.

23. Diary entry dated November 20th.

24. Diary entry dated December 4th.

CHAPTER FIVE

On Television

Just as Ted Ray seemed initially to be averse to radio, so, following his success in that medium, he expressed extreme doubt as to his embracing television. Reporting that Terry-Thomas had no interest in a career in television, the *Daily Herald* (May 15, 1952) asked Ted Ray for his opinion, which he shared in some detail:

"I'm plumping for radio to last out this T-V boom, and I'm sticking to it. TV is a one-eyed thing demanding undivided attention. TV kills everything else in the house.

"[Radio] gets to more millions all over the country, gets into the Army, Navy and Air Force camps all over the world, gets into the hospitals and is a boon to the blind.

"People can listen to radio in the kitchen, the dining-room, the bath and even the car. It's a housewives' help, It is not staring at you, demanding all your faculties all the time."

In a more jocular fashion, Ted Ray asked of television, "What is it anyway? Just a washing machine with a couple of extra controls. Don't talk to me about TV. I had the use of a boarding house keyhole for years. Crafty, that's what I am…

"Whatever success has come to me has been worked for. That meant studying every step of the ladder before I stood on it. So it seems to me that it would be foolish to run out from 'steam' radio that has, after all, made my name known to millions who could never have seen me on the Music Halls…

"You know enough about me to remember that I made a name in Variety on the stage long before radio adopted me. It took several years of really tough going before my name crept up the bill to be in letters big enough to read across the pavement. Am I being old-fashioned in thinking that that was good experience? And there was a lesson in it for later?…

"Perhaps you begin to understand why I love sound radio. It has brought me a host of new friends and faithful listeners. We are very real to each other."[1]

In his autobiography, published in 1952, Ted Ray maintains that television can never completely take the place of radio.[2]

Ultimately, Ted Ray's television work is not comparable in quality or appeal to his career in radio. So perhaps he was correct in his negativity towards the new medium. However, *The Times* (November 9, 1977) praised his television style, noting,

"He had an almost blatant directness of approach that enabled him, at his best, to transcend a medium which often tends to limit the appeal of the funny man who needs to stand in front of an audience and talk directly to it."

When it did come time for Ted Ray to make his television debut, he noted, "Trouble is I'm a new boy at TV. I'm thinking of asking [son] Andrew for some hints. I know he'll help his poor old dad."[3] (At the age of fourteen, Andrew Ray had already appeared in four television plays.)

It was not until 1955, when the comedian was featured in his own program on television, *The Ted Ray Show*, broadcast on Saturday evenings, at peak viewing times, beginning May 21st. There were three further, sixty-minute episodes, and the show returned on April 28th, 1956, for a further four episodes. It was back on January 19th, 1957 for eight episodes, and again on January 25th, 1958, for five episodes. That same year, *The Ted Ray Show* returned on September 27th for three episodes, and there was also an extract on the BBC's Christmas Day show, *Christmas Night with the Stars*. Finally, *The Ted Ray Show* returned on January 31st, 1959, for four sixty-minute episodes.

In retrospect, it seems odd that a show could have such a long life — from 1955 through 1959 — and yet consist in its entirety of only twenty-eight episodes.

For the series beginning January 19, 1957, Robin Ray received a contract to appear on the show as a foil to his father. And for the first program in that series, Ted Ray composed a new song, "London's My Town."

Various writers were associated with the show, including Talbot Rothwell of "Carry On" fame and Terry Nation, best known for *Doctor Who* (for which he created the Daleks). All but the 1959 season were produced by George Inns. The emphasis was on a variety concept, with guest stars and stand-up comedy until 1958 when Kenneth Connor and Diane Hart joined the show as Ted Ray's brother-in-law and wife and *The Ted Ray Show* became more of a situation comedy.

The singing, husband-and-wife team of Pearl Carr and Teddy Johnson[4] were regulars on the show, and harmonica player Larry Adler proved he could be a good stooge in comedy skits with the star.

Diane Hart (1926-2002) has the distinction of playing Ted Ray's wife both on radio and television. She is an actress worthy of a book in her own right having worked in music hall and on the legitimate stage (including the original production of *The Chiltern Hundreds* and Terence Rattigan's *Who Is Sylvia?*). She had worked in television almost since its conception at Alexandra Palace; she invented the "Beatnix" corselet; and ran unsuccessfully for parliament.

The Stage (March 20, 1958) reviewed the March 15th, 1958, show, and was not overly impressed:

"There's no doubting whose show it was on Saturday evening — the Ted Ray Show. In eleven acts, six of them starred Ted Ray, and all those starring Ted Ray went on for a very long time — or at least they seemed to. Benny Hill can get away with this sort of stuff and more. Let's face it, Ted Ray can't...

"For some of the time Ted was 'corny,' and though this has almost became a term of abuse these wisecracks can be very funny. He was a little unfortunate in having a studio audience which missed many a little gem. In snatches he was genuinely funny — particularly in the milkmaid and farmer's boy duet with Kenneth Connor at the end."

The general opinion from the public — as reported in the December 14th, 1959, issue of the *Liverpool Echo* — was that *The Ted Ray Show* was the usual run-of-the-mill variety interlarded with unfunny sketches. Viewers were also beginning to wonder if Ted Ray actually enjoyed the show any more than they did.

In a somewhat unusual move, concurrent with the BBC production of *The Ted Ray Show*, the comedian went over to the competition, Associated Television (ATV) for six, forty-five minute shows titled *Hip, Hip, Who Ray*, broadcast from August 25th through September 29th, 1956. From the BBC, Ted Ray brought over Sid Colin and George Wadmore as his writers. The series was a mix of stand-up comedy, short skits and guest performers, such as the Malcolm Mitchell Trio, who sang, and the Kathryn Orly Trio, who danced.

Following *The Ted Ray Show*, the comedian was featured by the BBC in *It's Saturday Night*, a series of four, forty-five minute variety shows, which aired from September 19th through December 12th 1959. Guests included June Whitfield, Alan Randall, Frank Ifield, and Robin Ray. *It's Saturday Night* featured film parodies and husband-and-wife sketches with Ted Ray and June Whitfield. The latter recalls the show being transmitted live from the Shepherd's Bush Theatre during an extreme heat wave, and she kindly provides a sampling of two jokes from the show:

In the first, Ted had given up smoking.

> TED: Look at my hands, they're trembling. I won't be able to play the violin.
>
> JUNE: Might be an improvement.

In another, he is accused of being unfaithful after he receives a mysterious telephone call.

> TED: It was a wrong number. Someone wanting the maternity home. There's nothing in it.
>
> JUNE: Nothing in it? What would you say if a man phoned me and asked for the maternity home?
>
> TED: I would say it was a blooming miracle.[5]

The BBC also presented Ted Ray in a couple of single episode shows. On September 22nd, 1957, he was seen, alongside Joan Turner, in the thirty-minute *Ray's a Rat*, honoring the Grand Order of Water Rats (more about whom and Ted Ray's involvement with later). Ted Ray is credited with the script, alongside George Wadmore. On December 13th, 1957, the comedian starred in the thirty-minute *Friday the 13th*, a sketch show by John Junkin and Terry Nation, produced by George Inns, in which Ted Ray asked "Are You Superstitious?"

On June 18th, 1965, a pilot titled *Happy Family* was aired by the BBC, under the blanket heading of "Comedy Playhouse." It was the only actual television sitcom in which Ted Ray starred, as a television advertising executive, and had him appear as the only man in a household consisting of his wife and four daughters, Sid Hills and Dick Green were the writers. Daphne Anderson played the wife, and it was claimed, somewhat improbably, that she was his 27th wife on radio and television. The daughters were played by Lyn Pinkney, Mary Maude, Judith (Judy) Geeson, and Carla Challoner. Completing the cast were Janet Harrington as Ted Ray's secretary and Patrick Westwood and Robert Raglan as his office colleagues. No series ever materialized. *The Stage* (June 14, 1965) commented,

"This is mild and well-worn comedy for early Friday night viewing... This was bland and ubiquitous as custard, he shows to better advantage in material with sharpness and bite...It's hard to get excited by or to find fault with this kind of routine comedy."

There were other one-off shows: *One Good Turn* (BBC, March 10, 1965), *Ted's Turn Again* (BBC, November 20, 1965), *Hooray for Laughter* (ABC, March 12, 1967), and *Suddenly It's Ted Ray*, on which he recalled stars of the music hall (BBC, August 28, 1967).

The last received a long drawn-out review in *The Times* (August 29, 1967), and it is worth reprinting at some length because it so perfectly captures the essence of Ted Ray and his long-lasting appeal:

"While Mr. Ray continues, no-one should talk about the extinction of the solo 'stand-up comics'. His programme was an exercise in nostalgia which led him to impersonate a dozen music-hall stars with nothing in common but their success. It was an achievement to convey something of personalities as diverse as, for example, Gracie Fields, Randolph Sutton, and Billy Bennett, but between his impersonations Mr. Ray cheerfully delivered a series of jokes of such outrageous corniness that it was impossible not to laugh at them.

"Mr. Ray did not merely get away with half-a-dozen corny stories which few of us would dare to repeat, but, by apparently casual timing and a sense of personal enjoyment, persuaded the viewer that they were really extremely funny. If and when the solo funny man becomes extinct, we shall mourn him for a long time, not because there is anything regrettable about the popularity of 'situation comedy,' but because the man who laughs at the sort of person he is and the way in which he sees life has to be someone special.

"Mr. Ray persuades us that he is the mouthpiece of the average man, ebullient, down to earth, ready for to laugh uproariously at comic postcards.

"Of course, the persuasion is only half the truth — it depends on precisely the same skill that Mr. Ray used to suggest to a drabber world something of the impact Nellie Wallace had on our grandparents. He impersonates the average man's idea of the average man."

Perhaps in part as an effort to duplicate the success of *Does the Team Think?* on television, the BBC introduced *I Object*, featuring Jimmy Edwards as the judge and Charlie Chester and Ted Ray as counsel. The series was produced by Albert Stevenson, who also produced *It's Saturday Night*, as well as series in the 1950s featuring Vera Lynn, Ken Dodd and Charlie Chester. Thirty minutes in length, it ran for ten episodes beginning April 14th, 1965 on BBC-1. The show was devised by Ted Ray and Charlie Chester, along with Charles Hart, and featured four debates on each episode, based on Charlie Chester or Ted Ray objecting to various issues, such as the confusing number of traffic signs on roads. A plaintiff might be a wife objecting to her husband squeezing the toothpaste from the middle rather than the bottom.

As Charlie Chester recalled, the BBC's head of comedy at the time, Frank Muir, asked him to withdraw from the show as he didn't "spark" with Ted Ray or Jimmy Edwards. Chester refused. And the three men were asked basically to audition in an empty room at Broadcasting House, "which was like ringing the death knell of a comedy vehicle before it even started."[6]

Based on the same participants showing up on these types of programs, be they on radio or television, one has the distinct impression that only a very limited number of comedians possessed the intellectual capability not only to improvise but to improvise with any degree of intelligence or wisdom.

That same emphasis on improvisation was apparent in Ted Ray's last major television series, *Joker's Wild*, which ran to 147 episodes in nine series, and was produced by Yorkshire Television from December 1969 through November 1974. Unfortunately, the improvisation is not memorable in large part thanks to some of the comedians quite frankly being too old and the younger comedians simply not being funny. I find it rather ironic that the series was created by Ray Cameron[7], along with Mike King, and Ray Cameron just happens to be the father of Michael McIntyre, a modern comedian whom I find totally unfunny.

Borrowing ideas from two American series, *Stop Me If You've Heard This One* and *Can You Top This?*, *Jokers Wild* has two teams of three comedians coming up with jokes based on a subject chosen by the host, Barry Cryer. While the joke is being told, a member of the opposing team could ring in and finish the joke. Ted Ray, and sometimes Arthur Askey, served as team captains, and regulars on the show included Les Dawson and Ray Martine[8]. The first show featured Ted Ray, Les Dawson, Charlie Chester, Jimmy Edwards, Alfred Marks, and Roy Hudd.

The jokes simply are not funny, despite the comedians finding them hilarious. They can barely control their laughter, something with which the viewer has no problem. One joke from Ted Ray will suffice to prove my point:

"One word of advice. Never go around with a married woman unless you can go three rounds with her husband."

What a sad way to end a career on television.

Not that it was exactly the end. There was still *New Faces* which ATV broadcast out of its Birmingham studios, and which sought to introduce new talent in a competitive fashion. There were four judges on the show, which aired from 1973 through 1988, and Ted Ray was occasionally one of their number. He was a member of the panel for the show broadcast on January 11, 1975, which declared comedian Lenny Henry as the winner.

Just as an invitation to appear on *Desert Island Discs* was *de riguer* for the top stars of radio, so was the surprise of *This Is Your Life*, hosted by Eamonn Andrews, for those considered to be sufficiently famous and to entertain viewers at the BBC. Ted Ray has the distinction of appearing twice on the show.

On October 23rd, 1955, he was surprised by Eamonn Andrews at the BBC Television Theatre. On hand were Kitty Bluett, G.H. Elliott, sister Jean from California, sons Andrew and Robin, and from the Liverpool days, Harry Wardle. The second surprise visit took place on Ted Ray's doorstep. He was taken to Euston Road Studios and the show was recorded on February 19th, 1975, for airing, a week later, on February 26th. Present at that recording were Ben Warriss, Ben Lyon, Noele Gordon, Diana Dors, Patricia Hayes, Robin Ray and his wife, Susan Stranks, and, via a live link, Arthur Askey and Dickie Henderson. The special surprise guests, flown in by the BBC from Rhodesia, were Andrew Ray, his wife and son, Mark[9]. Initially, the BBC had planned to fly in sister Jean from California, but Sybil Ray persuaded them to substitute Andrew Ray and his family.

Aside from twice being the subject of *This Is Your Life*, Ted Ray was also a guest of the show honoring comedian Reg Varney, broadcast live on May 20th, 1970.[10]

1. "Steam Radio…I Love It Says Ted Ray."

2. Ted Ray, *Raising the Laughs*, p. 107.

3. Philip Phillips, "Andrew Will Give TV Tips to Dad," p. 4.

4. They finished second in the Eurovision Song Contest of 1959 with their song, "Sing, Little Birdie."

5. June Whitfield, *…and June Whitfield*, p. 126.

6. Charlie Chester, *The World Is Full of Charlies*, p. 223.

7. Ray Cameron (1938-1993) also wrote *The Kenny Everett Show* (1981-1985). He was born in Canada and died, a suicide, in Los Angeles.

8. Until watching some episodes of *Joker's Wild*, I was not familiar with Ray Martine (1928-2002), who seems to verge on the camp but not quite make it. Les Dawson would apparently refer to him as "fey Ray" while Ray Martine would compare Les Dawson to Quasimodo. The only remotely funny remark I can find relative to Ray Martine and *Joker's Wild* is from Barry Cryer who, when asked what had happened to the comedian, responded that he was running an antiques business in Newcastle, adding, "he always did work with antiques."

9. A recording of Mark Olden discussing the family appearance on *This Is Your Life* is available on YouTube.

10. Other celebrities on that show included Pat Coombs, Bernard Miles, June Whitfield, and Barbara Windsor.

Early Photograph from the 1930s.

Sybil Stevens (later Mrs. Ted Ray), circa 1932. COURTESY OF MARK OLDEN

The Musical Ray Family: Andrew, Sybil, Robin, and Ted.
COURTESY OF MARK OLDEN

The family on holiday in Nice. COURTESY OF MARK OLDEN

Kitty Bluett.

DEARIE
by Bob Hilliard & Dave Mann
Broadcast and Recorded
by
TED RAY AND KITTY BLUETT
ON COLUMBIA DB 9698
1/-
CAMPBELL CONNELLY & CO., LTD.,
10 DENMARK ST., LONDON W.C.2.
LAUREL MUSIC Co., NEW YORK.
Authorised for Sale in Europe (excluding Spain) and the
British Empire (excluding Canada and Australasia).

Helena *(1951) with Isabel Jeans, Flora Robson, John Gielgud, and Adelaide Hall.*
COURTESY OF THE CINEMA MUSEUM

Does the Team Think *with Richard Murdoch, Tommy Trinder, Jimmy Edwards, and host McDonald Hobley.* COURTESY OF THE CINEMA MUSEUM

Meet Me Tonight *with Kay Walsh*.

With Ronald Shiner and Gilbert Harding on the set of My Wife's Family.

The Crowning Touch *with Greta Gynt*.

Please Turn Over.

Please Turn Over *with Jean Kent and Joan Sims.*

With Max Bygraves, circa 1967. COURTESY OF MARK OLDEN

Ted and Sybil with son Andrew. COURTESY OF MARK OLDEN

With son Andrew.

With grandson Mark. COURTESY OF MARK OLDEN

Playing golf, 1971.

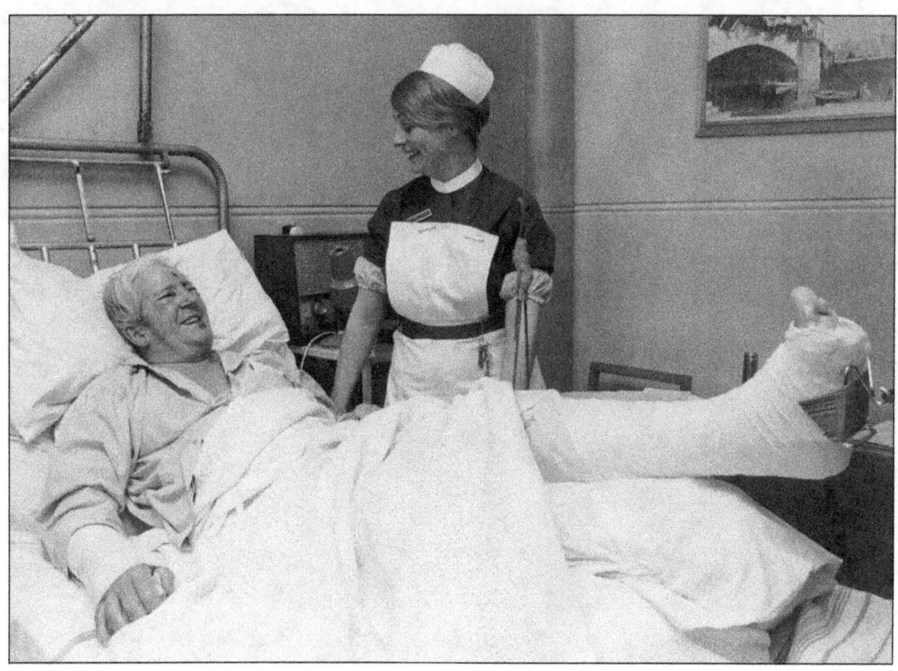

At the North Middlesex Hospital after his car crash, April 21, 1975.

CHAPTER SIX

On Screen

To all extents and purposes, Ted Ray's film career began — and ended — in the 1950s. It was not an auspicious one, and, truth be told, there is one production — *Meet Me Tonight* — which may be considered of any lasting worthiness.

Strange as it may seem, despite never have been heard on radio up to this point in his career, Ted Ray made his feature film debut in 1934 in a production titled *Radio Parade of 1935*. Production began in the autumn of 1934, with producer, British International Pictures, excitedly announcing that part would be shot in color. The film was shown to the critics in December of that year. The color process used only in the final reel is the British Dufay Color, an additive system, based on an earlier French invention by Louis Dufay. It is not particularly impressive and has problems so much so that there are those who wonder how it ever worked at all. It was later superseded, of course, by three-color Technicolor and Eastman Color, and was only used in two British feature films, *Radio Parade of 1935* and the 1939 production of *Sons of the Sea.*

The storyline of *Radio Parade of 1935* has Will Hay as William Garlon[1], director general of the National Broadcasting Group, appointing Clifford Mollison, as Jimmie Clare, head of complaints, to be the Group's program director and emphasize entertaining in its programming. Helen Chandler as Garlon's daughter is appointed secretary to the Clifford Mollison character. When Alfred Drayton, as Carl Graham, the head of an agency controlling variety performers, forbids their being heard of the Group's network, the Clifford Mollison character recruits amateur performers from the staff, and an eccentric inventor, A. Bird, played by Hugh E. Wright, unveils his latest creation, television, and the variety show is "televised" on gigantic screens throughout London's open spaces, including Trafalgar Square.

The Will Hay character is obviously a parody of the head of the BBC, Lord Reith, just as the National Broadcasting Group is a quite obvious parody. At one point, also, he messes with his hair, puts a comb under his nose, and gives a more than passable impersonation of Adolph Hitler. It should be acknowledged that the initials of the National Broadcasting Group, NBG, were generally understood at that time to stand for "No Bloody Good."

Highlights in the film, which is certainly entertaining and well-paced by director Alfred B. Woods, include the opening number, "I Wish You Good Morning," performed rather like a precision drill, and performances by music hall veterans, Lily Morris and Nellie Wallace as two charladies. Hollywood leading lady Helen Chandler is best remembered for playing Mina, opposite Bela Lugosi, in *Dracula*, and her appearance here is distinctly odd as she adds nothing to the film and can hardly have been considered a box office attraction. In her defense, she does give a good performance.

The high spot of *Radio Parade of 1935* is the last reel with two musical numbers in Dufay Color. The first features American jazz and blues performer, Alberta Hunter who was the first African American to play the role of Queenie opposite Paul Robeson in the 1928 London production of *Show Boat*, and was popular on both sides of the Atlantic. Her song, "Black Shadows," is quite extraordinary with its plea, "Lord can't you make them white." The lyrics continue,

> *"People regard me with hatred,*
> *Like I was covered in sin.*
> *Must I appear to be fated,*
> *All because of my skin?"*

It is a haunting, impassioned dirge, but is it politically correct or not, with its request from the singer to become white?

The second number is more traditional in approach, with Fred Conyngham, Peggy Cochrane, the Carlyle Cousins, and Teddy Joyce and His Orchestra performing "There's No Excusin' Susan."

A comment from *Motion Picture Daily* (December 28, 1934) is typical of critical response to the color: "At present it has shortcomings , the color being variable, with uneven flesh tints, ultra vivid greens and an imperfect white."

Ted Ray appears as the first of a group of variety performers relatively early in the film. The clip provides us with proof, if such was needed, that he was a first-rate violinist, at one point breaking into the Laurel and Hardy theme song, but he is not permitted to tell any jokes, thus making it an imperfect record of his music hall act from the 1930s. Also making cameo appearances in the film are two performers associated with the comedian. Stanelli doesn't play his violin here, but he does perform a number using car horns, which he dubbed a Hornchster, and which plays the chromatic scale. Certainly unique. Ronald Frankau performs what might be considered part of his cabaret act. It is interesting for the popular culture references to Anna May Wong and Josephine Baker, and, quite amazingly, what must be one of the earliest negative comments on screen relating to Adolph Hitler.

Radio Parade of 1935 opened at London's Regal Cinema, Marble Arch, in December 1934, and grossed $12,000.00 in its first week. As late as April 1935, it was playing at the Dominion Theatre, Tottenham Court Road. This despite *Variety* (January 15, 1935) describing the film as "good hoke — but not actually West End." *Motion Picture Daily* (December 28, 1934) described the story link as "strong and ingenious," adding, "The comedy angle is emphasized and the material is good and put over properly." *The Daily Mirror* (December 21, 1934) opined that "this picture is certain to start a cycle of films featuring radio stars, because the formula is box-office certainly." In fact, a month prior to the release of *Radio Parade of 1935*, another film, with a radio theme, *Death at Broadcasting House*, had been released. Singer Eve Becke was featured in both films, and the latter also boasts the presence of an African American singer, the great Elisabeth Welch.

All in all, *Radio Parade of 1935* is a good start to Ted Ray's career, confirming that by 1935 he was well-known to audiences. If only his appearance might have been double the length.

Fifteen years were to pass before Ted Ray made his second feature film, *A Ray of Sunshine*, filmed at the Viking Studios located in Kensington, and released in the summer of 1950. Producer Arthur Dent was the Russian-born founder of Adelphi Films, not the most prestigious of British production companies. Its director, Horace Shepard, had been making documentary short subjects for theatrical release since the 1930s. In 1948, he made a "B" picture, *The Flamingo Affair*, a crime drama that was his first feature-length production. Shepard's second feature was *Ray of Sunshine*, billed as "A Star Bright Sparkling Show." "Top line comedian of BBC *Ray's a Laugh* fame" Ted Ray introduces Wilson, Keppel and Betty (performing "Cleopatra's Nightmare"), impressionsist Janet Brown, Morton Frazer and His Harmonica Gang, and Ivy Benson and Her Girl Orchestra (which gets the most screen time).

The concept is a little unusual, making this not a typical variety bill with typical introductions. Ted Ray is first seen as the back end of a pantomime horse. "I've got grease paint in my veins. Sometimes I wish it was blood." He is kicked out after asking for advancement — perhaps becoming the front end of the horse. Having nowhere to stay, he sneaks into a gentleman's club and sleeps on an armchair there. In the morning, he awoken by a lanky maid, played by Lucille Gaye, who is both a dancer and contortionist, and their conversation is used to introduce the various acts, a couple of which are quite mediocre and unknown. Little person Morton Frazer and his harmonica gang are as irritating as their American counterparts, Borrah Minevitch and His Harmonica Rascals.

Ray of Sunshine, which was filmed under the title of *On with the Show*, is not an unpleasant way to pass an hour, thanks largely to the presence of Wilson, Keppel and Betty. Ted Ray's "performance" is adequate if not great. Unfortunately, his jokes are not funny, and there is too much emphasis on alcohol consumption. "Are you married, Mr. Ray?" asks the maid. "Certainly," he responds, "Do you think I drink for pleasure?"

Ted Ray's next feature film appearance is his most important, in part because it shows him to have talent as an actor, albeit somewhat playing himself. It came about, he writes in his autobiography, as a result of his driving actress Valerie Hobson home after she had participated with him in judging an unidentified competition. Although later married to John Profumo, one of the central characters in a sex scandal involving Christine Keeler, at that time Valerie Hobson had, for a number of years, been the wife of producer Anthony Havelock-Allan. Ted Ray, Valerie Hobson and her husband enjoyed each other's company for a couple of hours, although the comedian notes there was no business discussion.

A few weeks later, Anthony Havelock-Allan telephoned Ted Ray, telling him that he was producing a screen adaptation of three stories from Noel Coward's theatrical anthology, *Tonight at 8:30*, and he would like the comedian to star in the first of the stories, *The Red Peppers*, playing George Pepper, opposite Kay Walsh as Lily Pepper. "With my background," wrote Ted Ray, "I knew that in all humility the casting was right."[2]

Tonight at 8:30 had been a cycle of one-act plays by Noel Coward, presented on the West End and New York stage in 1936 and 1937 as starring vehicles for the playwright and Gertrude Lawrence. The ten plays were produced in groups of three, and three became feature films in their own right: *The Astonished Heart*, *We Were Dancing*, and *Still Life* (which was adapted by Coward as *Brief Encounter*).

The screen adaptation, retitled *Meet Me Tonight*, although the original title was used for the American release, begins with *The Red Peppers*, followed by *Fumed Oak* and concluding with *Ways and Means*. *Fumed Oak* had Stanley Holloway walking out on his miserable family life as represented by daughter, wife and mother-in-law. *Ways and Means* concerns a penniless aristocratic couple who force themselves on various acquaintances as house guests. The couple is played here by Nigel Patrick and Valerie Hobson, neither of whom can do much with what is basically weak material.

In *The Sketch* (September 24, 1952), the doyenne of British film critics, C.A. Lejeune, who dismisses Ted Ray as "a variety star," wrote, "Their combined effect is often entertaining, but a bit cruel, and generally rampageous and rowdy. I can't help feeling they may be a disappointment to anyone with a marked partiality for the plays."

In the *Daily Mirror* (September 12, 1952), Donald Zec was dismissive of the production, announcing, "This film laughs too loudly at its own jokes." In the British fan magazine, *Picturegoer*, Elizabeth Forrest was most enthusiastic:

"He [Ted Ray] proves that there are no anti-radio-comic gremlins that a shrewd director can't vanquish, and that there are no jinxes that a competent script can't exorcize.

"Certainly Ray had been a lot luckier with his material than Sid Field, Tommy Handley, Arthur Askey and the other top favorites who never quite succeeded in charming the movie camera as they charmed the microphone and the live theatre audiences. There is no element of luck, though about Ted Ray's handling of dialogue, gags and 'business.'

"It is as accomplished and expertly times as only a seasoned professional trouper could make it…

"That the sketch stands is a fine tribute to a fine company — particularly in the movie newcomer, Ted Ray, who seems to have found his screen legs at last. It should take away the bitter taste left behind by his earlier excursion into screen comedy, *Ray of Sunshine*, which was dissolved into a shower of unhappy raindrops."[3]

Anthology films were relatively popular at this time, with four of Somerset Maugham's shorts stories brought to the screen in 1948 as *Quartet*, and a further three filmed in 1950 as *Trio*, with an introduction by the author. A further three were adapted the following year as *Encore*. One of the stories comprising the latter release, *Winter Cruise*, was directed by Anthony Pelissier, and he also directed *Tonight at 8:30*. As *Variety* (September 17, 1952) described the film, it is "better class although somewhat dated entertainment," intended for a very middle-class cinema audience. "Short on excitement but funny and trenchant enough for many tastes," as the *New York Times* described it.

Wearing a ginger wig to match the red hair of his leading lady, Ted Ray is perfect casting. He can deliver a gag and make it live for the movie audience and watch it die before the stage audience of the film. "This act was good enough for my Mum and Dad, and it's good enough for you," says George Pepper to wife Lily, And that just about sums up the problem for this second-rate variety act, playing second-rate theatres, with a conductor who drinks beer while leading the orchestra during their act. Brilliantly played by Martita Hunt is Miss Grace, a one-time, famed star of the legitimate theatre, very much down on her luck to be appearing on the same bill and drowning her sorrows in alcohol. It all ends in tragedy and slapstick. "The…story calls for a 'poor show' by the song-and-dance team, and Ted and Kay 'do their worst," reported the *Daily Mirror* (February 20, 1952).

Shot in Technicolor over a two-week period at Pinewood Studios, the film's biggest problem for Ted Ray was that he and Kay Walsh had to perform two carefully staged and strenuous dance routines, "Has Anybody Seen Our Ship, the H.M.S. Peculiar" and "Men about Town." Luckily, they had the guidance of dance director Freddie Carpenter (1908-1987), who had choreographed "The 'Ampstead Way" number for the ill-fated 1946 British Technicolor musical, *London Town*.

Kay Walsh presumably had no problem with the dance routines as she had commenced her career in the late 1920s and early 1930s as a dancer. In fact, she once commented that she could not remember a time when she did not dance. Ted Ray was immensely lucky in having such a talented leading lady for his first real screen appearance. Kay Walsh (1911-2005) had the equally good fortune to work with her first husband, David Lean, in many great British films, including *In Which We Serve*, *This Happy Breed*, and *Oliver Twist*, for which she wrote the opening sequence.

Also in 1952, Ted Ray was seen in another film, his cameo appearance in which is obviously a gimmick, but one that works well. *Escape by Night* may well be described as a British film noir, which makes good use of exterior scenes, but which contains stereotypical characters and a stereotypical 1950s storyline. Basically, Bonar Colleano is an alcoholic crime reporter who goes on the run with a gangster, holing up in an abandoned theatre. The gangster, quite incredibly, is played by Sid James, using a fake Italian accent. His appearance alone is worth the price of admission, and, truth to tell, if one did not associate him with the later "Carry On" films, one would not be inclined to snigger at his performance. Unfortunately, watching him perform, all one can think about is that four years later he is to play a Western villain opposite Arthur Askey in *Ramsbottom Rides Again*. The climactic fight sequences between him and Bonar Colleano is a little slow — the direction at times is sluggish — and his being killed by his own gun is convenient.[4]

In the theatre, the two characters meet a ten-year-old boy, played by Andrew Ray, who is convinced the two men are secret service agents. Andrew Ray's father is played by Ted Ray, introduced on a single title card with the words, "And Guest Star Ted Ray." Again, if he was not already known as a comedian, audience could easily accept Ted Ray in this characterization. He has six scenes — probably two days work — playing opposite Avice Landone as his wife, and acquits himself well. The Andrew Ray character is severely injured in a fall during a rooftop chase, and, curiously, the film provides no indication as to whether he recovers or whether he is a cripple for life.

Playing Sid James' girlfriend and stereotypical nightclub singer is Egyptian-born Simone Silva, best known for appearing topless on the beach at the Cannes Film Festival with Robert Mitchum, rather than for minor films in which she appeared. Bonar Colleano was an American-born actor whose entire career was in British films, in which he was generally featured as a wisecracking Yank. *Escape by Night* is written and directed by John Gilling, who, unfortunately, is best remembered for the direction of *Vampire over London/Mother Riley Meets the Vampire*, also produced in 1952, and which starred Bela Lugosi and Old Mother Riley (Arthur Lucan).

The writer most associated with the "Carry On" films is Talbot Rothwell, and it was Talbot Rothwell who was partially responsible (along with director Gilbert Gunn) for the script of Ted Ray's next film, *My Wife's Family*. The source material was a 1920s farce written by American vaudeville comedian and monologist Fred Duprez, which was so popular that it had been filmed in Britain in 1931 and 1941, in Sweden in 1932, and in Finland in 1933. The plot, such as it is, concerns an interfering mother-in-law, played by Fabia Drake, who misunderstands her son-in-law's (Ted Ray) comments regarding a baby grand piano and believes he is discussing an illegitimate child, a misunderstanding enhanced with the arrival of the son-in-law's former girlfriend, played by Gloria Marsh. Joining Ted Ray as his wife is Diane Hart, who had played the same role both on radio and television. All good promotional material.

The Stage (February 2, 1956) wrote, hopefully but with no factual evidence, that "When *My Wife's Family* hits the cinema screens, Ted Ray will show how good an actor he is." When the film was first seen on television in 1970, the *Daily Mirror* (July 4, 1970) wrote of jokes bristling in a field of corn.

Diane Hart and Ted Ray were reunited for *The Crowning Touch*, released in the summer of 1959. The film is a slight, whimsical tale of a hat, "the crowning touch" of the title that has been ordered but not picked up by a customer at an expensive hat shop. The assistants in the shop come up with various ideas as to why it remains uncollected. Aside from Diane Hart, the film features an array of stalwarts of British cinema of the period, including Greta Gynt, Griffith Jones, Sydney Taffler, Dermot Walsh, Irene Handl, Max Bacon, and Allan Cuthbertson. The director, David Eady, was quite busy from the late 1940s through the early 1980s, but he directed nothing of note.

The Crowning Touch was released on the lower half of a double bill with the Sal Mineo/Gary Crosby vehicle, *A Private's Affair*.

So far in his film career Ted Ray had managed to stay out of the clutches of the producer of the "Carry On" films, Peter Rogers, but his luck ran out in 1959, when he was signed for the leading role of acting head master William "Wakie" Wakefield in *Carry On Teacher*, the third in the series. It was described by one modern commentator as being "as close to a gentle Ealing comedy that the Carry Ons ever got." He joined the regular "Carry On" of that time period, Kenneth Williams, Kenneth Connor, Charles Hawtrey, Leslie Phillips, Joan Sims, and Hattie Jacques. The original screenplay was not by Talbot Rothwell, but by Norman Hudis, who worked on some six "Carry On" films, and whose scripts are never quite as bawdy as those of the former. The director, as per usual, was Gerald Thomas. As with all the "Carry On" films, the production was shot at Pinewood Studios, with Drayton Green Primary School. West Ealing, serving as the location for Maudlin Street School.

The film opens with Ted Ray's character announcing to the staff that he is applying for a new position and that the Ministry of Education is sending a child psychiatrist (Leslie Phillips) and a school inspector (Rosalind Knight) to visit the school in a study of child behavior and staff control. The new job is in jeopardy if there is a negative report, and when the pupils hear this, they decide to sabotage the headmaster's chances. They like him too much and want him to stay. Eventually, the headmaster learns the truth behind the sabotage, is so touched by the affection of the pupils that he decides to stay. Presumably that he doesn't like caning has something to do with the pupils liking for him. There is almost a sentimental quality to the production, although it is certainly not played up until the end and instead there is a multitude of silly pranks (putting alcohol in the teachers' tea, having the Joan Sims' character split her shorts and show her knickers, etc.) and dubious jokes.

Ted Ray seems to be taken with the use of some comic gestures, such as placing his face in the palm of his hand, rather in the manner of Oliver

Hardy. He is forced to wriggle around, and join in what he appears to be a parody of the conga, along with the other adults, after the headmaster's study has been liberally drenched with itching powder. Off the set, Ted Ray displayed his humorous side by letting down the tires of Kenneth Connor's jaguar on the first day of filming. All is perhaps forgiven by the strong show of emotion Ted Ray expresses after Hattie Jacques has revealed to him the reason behind the behavior of the pupils.

As Donald Edgar, the film critic for the *Evening Standard* (September 3, 1959), wrote, "in those few moments Ted Ray represented what makes teaching pay: not money, but love."

In his autobiography, Kenneth Williams writes,

"I remember how we all sat in a circle of chairs on the set listening to Ted telling story after story with astonishing expertise. He had a mind for jokes like a file index and he vocalized characters so that you were entertained all the way to the tagline. That's the sure art of story-telling. The ones who can't do it are the ones who leave you thinking, 'Oh get to the end, for heaven's sake.'"[5]

Kenneth Williams wrote of its being a happy company, and that Peter Rogers and Gerald Thomas hosted a dinner in honor of the actors when the film was completed. Ted Ray delivered a speech entirely in verse.

Carry On Teacher opened at London's Plaza Cinema on September 3rd, 1959. The posters promised, hopefully, "You roared at *Carry On Sergeant*, howled at *Carry On Nurse*, you'll be convulsed by *Carry On Teacher*." The *Daily Herald* (September 4, 1959) reported, "the formula as before…Vulgar, lively fun." *Variety* (September 2, 1959) was surprisingly enthusiastic:

"An unabashed collection of uninhibited gag situations and dialog… Some of the gags are telegraphed but the cheerful impudence with which they are dropped into the script is completely disarming…Ray, playing straighter than most of his colleagues, gives a pleasant performance…a picture which knows precisely what target it is aiming at and, within its simple terms of reference, is a winner."

Peter Rogers wanted to sign Ted Ray up as a regular in the "Carry On" series, but the comedian determined the money was inadequate, something of which Kenneth Williams constantly complained. In his place, Peter Rogers signed Sid James. Happily we, the audience, along with Ted Ray himself have been spared the humiliation that he would doubtless have faced had he become permanently associated with the series.

Less than a decade later his career as a film star — if such he may be described — came to an end with *Please Turn Over*, which reunited Ted

Ray with producer Peter Rogers, director Gerald Thomas, screenwriter Norman Hudis and actors Leslie Phillips, Charley Hawtrey[6] and Cyril Chamberlain (who had played the school janitor in *Carry On Teacher*). As *Variety* described them, "good British character and feature players who have plenty of opportunities." The film is based on a 1954 play, *Book of the Month*, by Basil Thomas.

Released in the winter of 1959, *Please Turn Over* is a surprisingly entertaining and in some respects charming little film about a seventeen-year-old daughter (played by Margaret Lockwood's daughter Julia) who writes a *Peyton Place*-like novel, *Naked Revolt*, containing loosely-based portraits of her family: her chief accountant father (Ted Ray), who is presented as a womanizer, having an affair with his secretary, and embezzler; her mother (Jean Kent), who is having an affair with her driving instructor, Uncle Willie, identified as the daughter's biological father; her aunt, who is presented as an alcoholic; and the local doctor, for whom the aunt works, who has relationships with most of his female patients.

The audience is introduced to the content of *Naked Revolt* as the parents read it side-by-side. Despite the presence of so many from the "Carry On" series, *Please Turn Over* contains none of the vulgarity or crudity to be found there. It is unfortunate that the original poster for the film seems to be in the "Carry On" tradition, featuring a scantily-clad caricature of the daughter, and describing the film as a "titillating tale."

"I made it all up" proclaims the daughter but that does not stop the residents of this middle-class suburb from identifying all the characters as her family. Her impetus has been to make people face the reality of their lives, and only when the doctor threatens to sue does father Ted Ray describe his daughter as "the only real cause for pride and fame in this family."

Ted Ray proves himself a more than competent actor, at ease with this middle-class, pipe-smoking persona, identified first at the breakfast table as an obnoxious, irritable father who is quick to apologize to his daughter as the two drive to work. At times, the diction seems overly perfect and not really believable, and this somewhat hurts one's response to the film. Ted Ray and Jean Kent (a dramatic actress who had played in comedies opposite Arthur Askey and Tommy Trinder earlier in her career) demonstrate how well they can inter-react with each other, particularly as they argue over the content of the book and their daughter.

"Ted Ray gives his best film performance as the father who, in the novel, turns into a rake while Miss Kent is poised and assured as the wife," wrote *Variety* (January 20, 1960). Curiously, the paper praised what now seems the weakest and overly-long comedy sequence of "Uncle Willie" (Lionel

Jeffries) teaching the wife how to drive, describing it as "a masterpiece of comic reaction."

In his films, Ted Ray certainly ran the full gamut — from the sophistication of Noel Coward to the insistent vulgarity of the "Carry On" titles. He even made a brief, and successful, appearance in a British *film noir*. Basically, it was not an area of his career of which he might be particularly proud, but, then, there is nothing here of which to be deeply ashamed.

1. Various internet sources claim that characters in the film refer to the Will Hay character as Mr. Garland. This is simply not true. His name is quite distinctly pronounced "Garlon".

2. Ted Ray, *Raising the Laughs*, P. 171.

3. Elizabeth Forrest, "Threesome," pp. 19, 26.

4. He does not die in a hail of police bullets as claimed in internet references.

5. Kenneth Williams, *Just Williams: An Autobiography*, p. 108.

6. Despite his role being very small, Charles Hawtrey receives special billing in the credits.

CHAPTER SEVEN

The 1950s and Onwards — And Always Busy

Aside from radio, television and later films, Ted Ray continued to be active in other mediums and with other activities. Indeed, there were times when he actually worked simultaneously it would appear in more than one medium. For example, on Saturday, September 27th, 1958, he could be seen on television starring live in the first edition of *The Ted Ray Show*, and heard on the BBC Home Service introducing *Variety Playhouse*. The latter, which starred Cicely Courtneidge and Jack Hulbert, along with Ronnie Barker and Patricia Hayes, was, of course, pre-recorded.

Between 1948 and 1952, he was on stage at three Royal Command Performances at the London Palladium and the London Coliseum. The first, on November 1st, 1948, was headlined by Ted Ray's buddy, Danny Kaye, who made quite a hit, along with the Bernard Brothers and their unique style of impersonation. A surprise hit of the show was a teenage Julie Andrews, who had a solo spot towards the end of the first half and reappeared at the end to sing the National Anthem. It was also a sad night in that it marked the last appearance of music hall star, Nellie Wallace.

Ted Ray delighted the audience, with his performance described as "mercurial" by the *Daily Herald* (November 2, 1948). His first words on stage were "I've been in the business forty years and now I'm down to doing a one-night stand." The previous week, Ted Ray had been appearing with ventriloquist Senor Wences at the Tivoli Theatre, Hull, evidence of his non-stop performing. The following year, the Royal Command Performance took place not at the London Palladium, but the London Coliseum, on November 7th, with Maurice Chevalier headlining, and Ted Ray again received enthusiastically, although the occasional silence after a gag had him asking the audience to "see the jokes a little more quickly, please." Maurice Chevalier returned for the November 4th, 1952 Royal Command Performance at the London Palladium, with a cast including Ted Ray, the Crazy Gang, Gracie Fields and Norman Wisdom. The Queen pronounced it "a lovely show."

In advance of the June 1953 Coronation — in fact, considerably in advance of the Coronation — the BBC in February of that year hosted a *Royal Command Performance Radio Show*, with its biggest radio stars including, of course, Ted Ray, along with Ben Lyon and Bebe Daniels, Peter Brough, and the cast of *Take It from Here*, Jimmy Edwards, Dick Bentley and Joy Nichols.

In acknowledgment of his being a star of both radio and television, Ted Ray was also present as co-host, with Terry-Thomas of the BBC's *Coronation Music Hall*, billed as television's biggest-ever variety show and broadcast on May 16, 1953. Joining the hosts were Arthur Askey, Norman Wisdom, Tessie O'Shea, and Trinidadian pianist Winifred Atwell.

As well as doing his patriotic duty by performing in front of the Royal Family, Ted Ray also did his patriotic bit by entertaining the troops, as a member of Combined Services Entertainment (CSE), during the Korean War in September and October 1952, stopping en route in Hong Kong to entertain wounded soldiers at the General Hospital. He actually asked one of the soldiers who was badly burned and blackened on the face to give him an impersonation of Al Jolson.[1]

The comedian left the U.K. on September 22nd, with six other entertainers, and was scheduled to put on at least three, ninety-minute shows daily, with flights of up to 100 miles between venues over a period of five weeks. Prior to leaving for the Far East, that summer Ted Ray had embarked on a provincial tour, attended the premiere of *Meet Me Tonight*, and taken a brief holiday in Juan les Pins.

The British War Office would appear to have been somewhat late in realizing how much the presence of popular entertainers might help the morale of its troops in Korea and Malaya. Singer Donald Peers had offered to entertain but initially had been rejected by the War Office until it reversed its decision in June 1952. Ted Ray was next selected to go, after Donald Peers, with more acts, including Frankie Howerd and Bill Kerr, promised later for the troops.

Ted Ray spoke of his experiences on the BBC Light Programme on November 3rd, 1952, and a syndicated column, "With Our Boys in the Far East" was published in local newspapers while the comedian was still overseas.

Earlier, on a much less dangerous mission, in March 1950, he had flown to Germany to entertain troops there. Also part of the troupe were Cyril Fletcher, Diana Dors, Bob Monkhouse, Geraldo and His Orchestra, and Denis Goodwin, who also wrote the scripts.

The comedian had been asked if he might perform for badly wounded soldiers in hospitals in the U.K., but the mission was too emotional a one:

"I'd love to go and do a show for the lads…, but I just can't face it…to see all those poor devils make me feel ill, and I'd probably do more harm than good."[2]

The one charitable concern with which Ted Ray was closely associated was the Grand Order of Water Rats. This oddly named organization was a major show business charity, although its name means very little to most people today and its membership is not quite as heavy with prominent entertainment figures.

Its founding goes back to the late 1880s, when Joe Elvin was part owner of a racing pony called the Magpie. One morning, a bus driver encountered Joe and Magpie in the pouring rain. He asked what was the pony's name, saying that it looked like water rat. Magpie became Water Rat, and celebrating its success in the summer of 1889, Joe Elvin took a party of friends out to dinner and suggested they call themselves "Pals of the Water Rat."

And so, as a result of a rather long-winded and uninteresting beginning, the Grand Order of Water Rats became established as a charitable organization, with the motto of "Philanthropy, Conviviality and Social Intercourse." The first King Rat in 1890 was Harry Freeman, noted for his comic songs such as "The Giddy Little Girl Said No." He was succeeded as King Rat by a legendary entertainer of the music halls, Dan Leno, serving in 1891, 1892 and 1897.

Ted Ray was initiated into the Grand Order of Water Rats on March 5, 1933, being Water Rat No. 338. He was proposed for membership by two very obscure comedians, Sammy Shields and Dusty Rhodes. Glaswegian-born Sammy Shields (1874-1933) made his variety debut at the Holborn Empire in June 1905. He was billed as "The Football Comedian," and even made recordings of his monologues at football matches, including Rangers versus Celtic in 1923. Dusty Rhodes was variously billed as "The Comedy Merchant," "The Tramp Comedian" and "The Great Singing Comedian."

Ted Ray served as King Rat in 1949 and again in 1964. Tommy Trinder has been King Rat in 1963 and again in 1965. Other King Rats include Will Hay (1931 and 1940), Ben Warriss (1953, 1961 and 1962), Joe Church (1975) and Danny La Rue (1987).

Membership of the Water Rats is by invitation only, and until the early 1930s it was limited to male member of the variety profession. There are American members, including, of course, Danny Kaye, Olsen and Johnson, and Stan Laurel and Oliver Hardy. Ted Ray devotes some six pages to the organization in his autobiography and obviously regards his elevation to King Rat as one of the greatest honors in his career.

Ted Ray's comic stature led to his being approached to advertise a variety of products. The earliest of printed advertising featuring Ted Ray would appear to be for Star Double Edge Razor Blades in the summer of 1950. In April 1955, he was joined by wife Sybil and son Andrew promoting Gibbs Toothpaste in a tin, better known as Gibbs Dentrifice. In October of the same year, he could be found advertising Services sports watches. And in June 1956, Ted Ray was proclaiming the benefit of owning a Brownie 44a Camera.

The comedian was also promoting himself in 1952 through publication of what was claimed to be his "autobiography," *Raising the Laughs*. It is a curious book in that it seems deliberately to avoid too many dates, including Ted Ray's date of birth

In the early 1950s, the publishing house of T. Werner Laurie, which in its early years had published the likes of Joseph Conrad, Upton Sinclair and W.B. Yeats, realized that the radio-listening public might well be willing to purchase and read autobiographies from its favorite stars, including Wilfred Pickles (*Personal Choice*, 1950), Donald Peers (*Pathway*, 1951), and Jimmy Edwards (*Take It from Me,* 1953). Jimmy Edwards actually wrote *Take It from Me*. That placed his book significantly above the other T. Werner Laurie celebrity autobiographies, all of which, including the Ted Ray volume, were "ghosted" by Gail Pedrick[3] who worked in the BBC's Variety Department.

The Ted Ray autobiography is somewhat unusual in that it seems the comedian did not provide his ghostwriter with enough material, and so there is virtually an entire chapter devoted to "fan worship," the study of which is described as a hobby of Gale Pedrick, and which has nothing really to do with Ted Ray.

Whether the comedian actually wrote it is unknown, but his name did appear as the author of a weekly, Saturday column, "Ray's a Story" in early 1957 in the *Liverpool Echo*, and later, "Ray's a Laugh," in the same newspaper at the end of 1959.

In 1963, Ted Ray published a book titled *My Turn Next*, which might also be considered an alternate biography, with his being brought up by his Uncle Reuben and Aunt Lucy. There are some factual references, such as the London Music Hall and Will Fyffe, but otherwise the book is nothing more than a series of rambling stories relating to alcohol, and all of it unamusing.

Throughout the 1950s, Ted Ray continued with live appearances just as he had done in the 1930s and 1940s. In July 1952, he was at the Floral Hall, Scarborough, with frequent partner, Joan Turner, along with Peter Sellers from *Ray's a Laugh*; the following month, the three were on stage at the Winter Gardens, Eastbourne. When star Max Bygraves had to leave the cast of *Wonderful Time* at the London Hippodrome to fulfill pantomime commitments, Ted Ray took his place. There was a summer season at Great Yarmouth in 1954. In July 1955, he was at the Capitol Theatre, Aberdeen, with female impersonator, Mrs. Shufflewick, "broadminded to the point of obscenity." He was still appearing at the London Palladium. For example, in April 1955, he was headlining there with singer Dickie Valentine. Also on the bill was strongwoman Joan Rhodes, whose act consisted primarily of her tearing telephone books in half — just as she had done on the May 8th, 1957, broadcast of *The Ted Ray Show*.

It was claimed that Ted Ray had appeared at the London Palladium more times than any other comedian except for Joe Church, a stand-up comedian whose name is unknown today.

1. Created in 1946 by the U.K. government to replace E.N.S.A. and provide live entertainment for army and R.A.F. personnel.

2. Charlie Chester, *The Grand Order of Water Rats: A Legend of Laughter*, p. 139-140.

3. Frank Gale Pedrick Harvey (1906-1970) was also a scriptwriter, whose work includes the first thirty-five episodes of the British version of *This Is Your Life*.

CHAPTER EIGHT

Robin and Andrew Ray

Ted Ray had two children, both of whom enjoyed careers of distinction in the entertainment field. "It makes me feel like a theatrical landlady, the house is full of pros," remarked Ted's wife, Sybil. "You've no idea what it's like. They all criticize each other — but we have fun. And not a swollen head among the three of them…no, not even Ted!"[1]

The oldest son, Robin, was born on September 17th, 1934, at 630 Fulham Road, Fulham. Andrew Ray was born on May 31st, 1939, at Onslow House Nursing Home in Southgate. Robin was educated at a private prep school, "The Hollies," and then the (at the time) all-boys Highgate School, whose headmaster, Geoffrey Bell, was a distinguished if somewhat austere former cricketer, awarded the military cross during World War One. Other "old boys" include poet Gerald Manley Hopkins, documentarian Paul Rotha, film director Adrian Lyne, and actor Roland Culver.

Andrew Ray attended prep school at Franklin House in Palmers Green. Andrew effectively left school when he was ten to become an actor. He was later privately tutored on various movie sets. He is quoted as saying, "My education really stopped at 10. How can you go back to school and remain unchanged when you're suddenly a film star."[2]

Sybil Ray might compare her household to a theatrical boarding house, but, in reality, she maintained quite strict control over her boys, more so than a theatrical landlady. Nor was the stringency of her rules limited to the children, with her once telling Ted Ray off for "leaving the soap dirty."

Robin Ray's wife, Susan, recalls,

"They always ate hugely well with the best food being very much part of their lives — and plenty of it. Always enormous roasts on Sundays — known in the family as 'blow-outs'. Sybil was the undisputed queen of her kitchen but in his later years Ted would rustle up a mean spaghetti Napolitan or Bolognese. They chose good restaurants both at home and on holiday and Ted loved high quality food and wine. They did have the 'feast chest' which was a huge tin of sweets which came out officially at weekends but was regularly raided with Sybil's encouragement.

"She was huge on treats but fairly tough on discipline. If angry she would (seriously) chase the boys round the kitchen with a broomstick.

"They always had dogs, which Sybil absolutely adored, and always fed very well with home cooking — hearts, liver, stewing steak, etc."[3]

"The first I knew about was a spaniel called Wheater. Then there was a mongrel/Irish terrier pup, bought by Syb on a walk, pestered by the boys, from a complete stranger on the Brighton prom [promenade]. Kelly was a complete reprobate and much loved. Then there was a Golden Labrador. Her last was a German shepherd 'Sheena.' All very much Sybil's. She adored dogs, and she walked, cared for and fed them amazingly."[4]

As to how strict Ted and Sybil were as parents, Susan Ray recalls,

"I would say on and off! Ted wouldn't stand any disrespect of Sybil and they pretty much maintained a united front. He did cover up for a few of the boys misdemeanours — broken windows and such. If they were suspected of lying they were made to swear on the huge family bible. Sybil was incredibly impetuous and would spoil them on huge shopping trips."[5]

She could be patient and kind, but she was also a very strong character — blunt," as grandson Mark recalls. Ted was shrewd with his money, whereas Sybil liked to go shopping, particularly to Harrods.

Politics

The family was split politically. Ted Ray typifies the "old school" of stand-up comics, who came from a working-class background, but were strongly conservative. They ranged from the moderate such as Ted Ray and Ken Dodd through the strong, such as Arthur Askey, to the reactionary such as Eric Sykes. Ted Ray died before Margaret Thatcher became prime minister in 1979, but he would, in all probability, have been a strong supporter of the Iron Lady.

While a number of vintage British comedians were right-wing in their politics, they did not insinuate their ideology into their act. Such is not true of current right-wing comedians, of which there are a handful. They stand out, in large part, because of the paucity of their number and because they seldom secure a significant audience. The BBC has a policy of encouraging conservative comedians to be heard on radio and television, usually on quiz shows and the like. The problem has been that the studio audience for these shows are not right-wing and the comedians often have a hard time persuading an audience to empathize with them.

Geoff Northcott grew up on a working-class council housing estate in South London — his mother was disabled and his father was a union man — but, his comedy is pro-Conservative and pro-Brexit. Although he is unknown in the U.S., Northcott has been named as one of the 100 most influential Conservative figures. Since 2013, Northcott has grown in stature as a comedian and also a political commentator, appearing on the BBC's *Question Time*. He certainly lives up to his publicity as "the UK's only declared Conservative comedian." However, his reputation and popularity will never surpass that of Ken Dodd, Arthur Askey or Ted Ray.

During the making of *The Betty Witherspoon Show*, on November 20th, 1972, Ted Ray had a confrontation with Miriam Margolyes:

MIRIAM: You'd say then would you that you come from a working class background?

TED: Yes.

MIRIAM: I can't understand why people like you aren't social-ists, all my friends are and we're from the middle-class.

TED: It's this wealth tax the Labor people would bring in. Why can't they let people with money have it? They've earned it.

MIRIAM: Who better to tax than the rich?

TED: But they've worked for it. And what do they do — they give it to those layabouts outside Labour Exchanges. I've seen them. They don't do anything.[6]

And so it went on...

Miriam Margolyes does not recall this altercation, but says she is sure it is true. "Ken Dodd, Arthur Askey, Ted Ray, I had arguments with all of them."[7]

There would be similar debates with Robin Ray, two eloquent men who loved verbally jousting.

As his son, Mark, points out in regard to his father, Andrew Ray:

"My dad...was indeed of the left and passionate in some of his com-mitments (though he was never ideological/had friends from across the political spectrum/and could take surprising positions on different issues)."[8]

Robin Ray would appear to have initially been conservative, but by the 1970s, he was a liberal, although probably not as left-wing as his brother. As he grew older, he moved more to the right. He became what is described as "a one-nation conservative." That is someone who believes in the preservation of established institutions and traditions within a democracy, while supporting social and economic programs that benefit the ordinary citizen.

At an early age, Robin Ray evinced an interest in an acting career and also developed a taste for classical music. After military service, he studied at the Royal Academy of Dramatic Art, and later became its chief technical instructor from 1961-1965. Earlier, he had made his West End stage debut in a 1960 production of *The Changeling*, a Jacobean tragedy first performed in 1622.

That same year, on January 25th, Robin Ray married Susan Stranks, a familiar figure on ITV as one of the presenters of a series for older children titled *Magpie*. Thames Television's somewhat more hip answer to the BBC's *Blue Peter*, its host from 1968 through 1974, Susan Stranks, was much admired by boys who were at that time on the cusp of adolescence. For Thames Television, Susan Stranks also devised and presented *Paperplay*, on air from 1974 through 1981. The couple have a son, Rupert.[9]

From August 28th through September 2nd, 1961, Robin Ray had starred, along with Dilys Laye, Fenella Fielding Anton Rogers in the Edinburgh Festival late night revue, *5 + 1*.

As early as December 27th, 1957, Robin Ray had appeared on the children's television show, *Crackerjack*, along with his father. Ray's major television break came in 1965, when BBC2 began airing *Call My Bluff*, an imported game show from the United States, created by Mark Goodson and Bill Todman and televised only briefly by NBC in 1965. Opposing team members were asked to define obscure words, with the help of illustrations provided by the cartoonist "Emmwood," while rival team members had the opportunity to guess which of the definitions were incorrect. One team was captained by writer Frank Muir and included actress Celia Johnson, while the other team was captained by actor Robert Morley and included *Daily Mirror* personal help columnist or "agony aunt," Marjorie Proops. Robin Day was, in the words of one journalist, "every young lady's ideal chairman.

The show was first broadcast on October 17th, 1965, and ran for twenty-four years. On August 3rd, 1972, BBC2 began broadcasting *Face the Music*, on which panelists were asked questions regarding classical music, with Joseph Clutch as chairman, and panelists including newsreader Richard Baker, *Punch* columnist Paul Jennings, David Attenborough, actress Joyce Grenfell, and, from the third show onwards, Robin Ray.[10] From 1972 through 1974, Robin Ray also hosted *The Movie*

Quiz, on which panelists, including Michael Parkinson and Sylvia Sims were asked questions relating to film history.

There were other shows, including *Music Now* (1969-1970) and *The Lively Arts* (1976-1977), all of which are notable for the intelligence of the concept and presentation. Robin Ray was never involved in anything on the air that was lightweight or frivolous. His presence was always a sign of quality.

In the 1980s, Robin Ray was involved in two theatrical ventures. With Cameron Mackintosh, he devised *Tomfoolery*, based on the satirical songs of Tom Lehrer, and also appeared in the original London production at the Criterion Theatre on June 5th, 1980. *The Times* (June 6, 1980) described Robin as "a suave compere…What he says is witty and well turned; but it converts Lehrer, the rough popular bard, into a bland entertainer." The show made a successful transition to New York, presented off-Broadway, and continues to be performed through the present. "The show is not without its intermittent pleasures," reported Frank Rich in the *New York Times* (December 15, 1981). In association with Andrew Lloyd Weber, Robin Ray wrote the musical, *Café Puccini*, which opened at Wyndham's Theatre on March 12, 1986, and has the distinction of being one of the few Andrew Lloyd Weber shows that was not a success.

Earlier, Robin Ray had been associated with another composer, Stephen Sondheim, when he was a member of the replacement cast for *Side by Side by Sondheim* at Wyndham's Theatre, beginning April 4th, 1977.

Robin Ray was noted for his encyclopedic knowledge of classical music. He could name not only the piece and the composer but also the opus number, and this led to his appearing regularly on the BBC's *Face the Music* (as mentioned) and also presenting *Robin Ray's Record Review* on Capitol Radio. It also led to his joining the commercial classical music station, Classic FM, from 1991 through 1997. Between 1966 and 1995, Robin Ray claimed that he had written and presented more than 1,000 programs for the BBC and commercial radio.

He also compiled for Classic FM a listing of 50,000 pieces of classical music, rated for popularity. When he left Classic FM this led to a lawsuit involving copyright in the listing, a lawsuit which Robin Ray won. He also wrote books associated with his musical knowledge: *Music Quiz* (1978) *Favorite Hymns and Carols* (1982) and *Words on Music* (1984).

It is Andrew Ray who is always recognized as the film star in the family, but, through the years, Robin appeared in a few films, often uncredited, *Passport to Treason* (1956), *The Young and the Guilty* (1958), *I'm All Right*

Jack (1959), *Sink the Bismarck!* (1960), *Carry On Constable* (1960), *Doctor in Love* (1960), *Watch Your Stern* (1960), and *A Hard Day's Night* (1964).

Sadly, Robin Ray died in Brighton, long before his time, of lung cancer on November 29th, 1998. He was only sixty-four.

Andrew Ray's introduction to the screen came about inadvertently thanks to brother Robin.

His father received a telephone call from Ben Lyon, who with his wife, Bebe Daniels, was based in London and at the time was working for 20th Century-Fox in the role of a senior casting director. He had been asked to cast a film that the Hollywood company was making in the U.K. Back in the 1930s, various Hollywood production companies had purchased so-called "quota quickies" from British producers to satisfy the government-enforced quota system that required a large percentage of films shown in theatres be British. After World War Two, Hollywood producers decided to produce films themselves not only for U.K. release, to satisfy the quota system, but also for worldwide distribution. Such films would be major productions with major Hollywood stars. M-G-M produced *The Miniver Story* (1950), Paramount produced *So Evil My Love* (1948), Walt Disney produced *Treasure Island* (1950), etc.

The first American film to be shot in the U.K. was *Escape* (1948). The producer was 20th Century-Fox, and it continued to make a number of films in Britain, including *The Mudlark*, which Ben Lyon was casting. The production starred Irene Dunne, badly cast and heavily made up as Queen Victoria, and concerned a young boy of the title, a mudlark, who searches the mud along the banks of the Thames for anything of value. One day, in 1875, he finds a cameo of Queen Victoria and because she looks like his mother, he decides to visit her at Windsor Castle. His appearance before the Queen persuades her to listen to the advice of her prime minister Disraeli (very well played by Alec Guinness) and to emerge from the seclusion caused by the death of Prince Albert and to show herself to her people. Sentimental fiction, from a novel by Theodore Bonnet, based on "the boy Jones," who, in the words of *The Times* (October 5, 1950), "had such a passion for breaking into palaces in the nineteenth century."

Ben Lyon remembered Robin Ray as a child and asked his father to bring him along to his Piccadilly offices with the possibility that he might be suitable for the title character. Ted Ray duly showed up, not only with his oldest son but also the youngest one, who had apparently come along for the ride. Ben Lyon immediately realized Robin was too old for the part, but was intrigued by Andrew despite his father assuring the actor/casting director, "he's so shy and self-conscious you wouldn't want him."[11]

Andrew was asked to speak a few words into a tape recorder. Two days later he was called in for a screen test. The test was sent to 20th Century-Fox head, Darryl F. Zanuck, in Hollywood, and within hours Andrew Ray was offered the role. (According to his father, Robin Ray was also given a part in the film, but he is uncredited and unrecognizable.)

The Mudlark began shooting at Shepperton Studios in May 1950, following completion of the Tyrone Power vehicle, *The Black Rose*. Jean Negulesco was the director, with Nunnally Johnson serving as both producer and screenwriter. The French-born, British-based Georges Périnal was cinematographer. It was a distinguished company, with the film enhanced by the presence of Finlay Currie (as John Brown), Anthony Steel and Constance Smith.

The film was selected as a Royal Command Performance at the Empire Theatre, Leicester Square, on October 30th, 1950. And then the controversy began in earnest. There were already whispers of annoyance that Britain's most famous ruler was being played by an American. Now it seemed that a film identified as American, although it was actually British, was chosen for a Royal Command Performance, an honor usually given only to a British film. "That it sailed through these two crises to triumph," commented *Variety* (November 8, 1950), "is, in itself, a tribute to its quality and sincerity. And, perhaps, also to the British sense of fair play."

Following the film, in what must have been a very long evening, was a stage presentation, featuring Marlene Dietrich, Claudette Colbert, Margaret Lockwood, Jean Kent, Valerie Hobson, James Stewart, Tyrone Power, Michael Redgrave, and Irene Dunne. Ted Ray appeared alongside his son in a sketch that he had specially written for the evening.

After the entertainment was finally over, the assembled company was introduced to King George VI and Queen Elizabeth. Princess Elizabeth, the late Queen, spoke with Andrew and told him how much she had enjoyed his performance. 'Thank you, your Majesty," he responded. "No, Andrew, not 'Your Majesty,' 'Your Highness,'" she answered. "But that's all right, we often make mistakes ourselves."

What a truly patronizing and pretentious comment to make to an eleven-year-boy. It is enough to have turned him into a leftist, anti-monarchist. And perhaps it did. It is more a comment one might expect from Princess Margaret. But then, perhaps, in her defense, Elizabeth was trying to be humorous.

The next day, the British critics were uniformly positive in their response to the film and Andrew's performance. "*The Mudlark* is not a great film, but it is very affective and attractive, and when all is said and done it stands on the magnificent performance of Alec Guinness as Disraeli," wrote Jympson Harman in *The Evening News* (October 31, 1950). A similar opinion was voiced by Ewart Hodgson in the *News of the World*,

"With 1950 nearing its end, I am convinced that there is little possibility of the screen offering a greater acting performance. The delicacy, the constraint, the detached urbanity he brings to the part had me transfixed as if I were a rabbit and he a ferret."

C.A. Lejeune wrote in *The Sketch* (November 22, 1950),

"Alec Guinness…is brilliant — no other word will do him justice. He can say volumes with the infinitesimal lift or droop of an eyelid. His speech in the House of Commons (straight out of *Hansard*) is as certain to move an audience as it is reputed to have swayed the members. *The Mudlark* may not be a memorable film, but it is certainly memorable in this one way — that it has educed from a British actor what is probably the finest performance of the year."

She declared Andrew Ray to be "just right." Jympson Harman wrote that Andrew Ray "is a genuine discovery for British films. Young Andrew speaks his cockney lines in a manner which should end for all time Hollywood's illusions in this matter."

The Times (October 31, 1950), described *The Mudlark* as "a hybrid," pointing out, "it is difficult to think of one [word] that can better describe a film made with American money in English studios with a leading American player and a predominantly English cast."

The Mudlark opened in New York at the Rialto Theatre, as the Christmas presentation, on December 25th, 1950, and was described by Bosley Crowther in the *New York Times* as "a warm and rewarding show." He continued,

"Properly, the honors for performance unqualifiedly go to little Andrew Ray, who plays the title role. In his wee face, he touchingly expresses the amazement and confusion of a humble guttersnipe caught in the stiff and ponderous meshes of an unsuspected trap. In small voice, he chirps the shocking candor and independence of a Cockney toff. And in his slight frame, he demonstrates the vigor and agility of all the world's young boys."

Astonishing praise for a ten-year-old boy with no acting experience, but who must, one feels, have learned much from his father — and benefited, it must be acknowledged, from the sympathetic direction of Jean Negulesco.

Unfortunately, there was little sympathy either from the audience or the critics for Andrew Ray's second performance — not on screen but on stage. It was at the request of Laurence Olivier that the young man be featured in the comedy, *The Happy Time*, which had been a success in New York, and which Olivier was now producing in London at the St. James's Theatre. A comedy by Samuel Taylor, adapted from a novel by Robert Fontaine, *The Happy Time* concerned a French-Canadian family in Ottawa of the 1920s. All were succeedingly odd, including Bibi, played by Andrew Ray, who was experiencing a sexual awaking and steals a nightdress from the maid because he wants to see her in the nude.

The Happy Time opened on January 30th, 1952, after a week in Edinburgh. It closed five weeks later. Heading the cast were Ronald Squire, Peter Finch, George Devine (who also directed), and Rachel Kempson.

Critics complained of Andrew Ray's French-Canadian accent. *The Stage* (February 7, 1952) wrote that he "has a very long part…and faces it bravely and likeably. But too often during the first performance his words were caught only after much ear-straining and sometimes not even then."

The gallery audience erupted in uproar at the play's close, having had difficulty hearing much of the play. As poor Andrew Ray stepped forward shyly to thank the audience for its applause, there were cries of "Shoot the author."

Through it all, Andrew Ray had the full support and encouragement of Ted Ray, and his mother was at the theatre every night acting as his companion and dresser. He learned how to change his acting style while on stage, varying the delivery of his lines.

(*The Happy Time* was filmed that same year, under the direction of Richard Fleischer, with Bobby Driscoll as Bibi, and participation from Charles Boyer and Louis Jourdan. It was also the basis for a 1967 musical of the same name by John Kander and Fred Ebb. Unlike *Cabaret* and *Chicago*, for which Kander and Ebb are also responsible, none of the songs are memorable.)

Andrew Ray was fast becoming Britain's leading child star — if not the country's only child star. No sooner had *The Happy Time* closed than he was signed for his second screen appearance in what was to be the country's second "X" rated film, *The Yellow Balloon*, which just happened to be also the second film directed by J. Lee Thompson (who also wrote the screenplay and was to go on to direct *The Guns of Navarone*, among many other successful efforts). *The Yellow Balloon* was released in the U.K. in December 1953, but did not reach the United States until October of the following year, when it was first screened at the Normandie Theatre, New York.

In the *New York Times* (October 15, 1954) Bosley Crowther wrote of "the noted disposition of the British to make movies about frightened kids and make them with interesting mixtures of menace and child psychology" as with *The Yellow Balloon*. Its plot concerns twelve-year-old Frankie in London's East End (played by Andrew) who has lost the sixpence he was given by his father to buy a yellow balloon. He grabs the balloon of a friend, Ronnie, and in the chase that ensues, the latter falls to his death in a bombed-out house. Len, crook on the run (played by William Sylvester) sees what has happened and basically blackmails Frankie into stealing from his parents (Kenneth More and Kathleen Ryan) rather than be reported to the police. After being used as a decoy in a pub robbery in which Len kills the landlord, Frankie is forced to flee with Len chasing him through an abandoned underground station. As the American trade paper *Variety* (February 23, 1953) noted, *The Yellow Balloon* is basically the study of an innocent child — well not so innocent — who falls into the clutches of a modern-day Fagin.

The film was shot in black-and-white, and, of course, the color of the balloon is never actually seen. Through it all, Andrew Ray manages to look wide-eyed and nervous as he is forced into acts he does not wish to perform. *Variety* wrote that "the boy plays the part almost on a single key but his almost static expression captures the story's spirit." And, as Bosley Crowther pointed out, children should speak up rather than harbor their fears. But they don't. Otherwise we would not have films such as this.

For a young boy, the 1950s must have been exciting times for Andtew Ray. He was busy on screen, on stage, and then television. From contemporary reports, he enjoyed his new life as a juvenile leading man, greeting it with a degree of precociousness mixed with enthusiasm. He seems to have enjoyed the give-and-take with his father as they vied with each other as to who was the biggest star. And Andrew would seem to be the winner here, although on *Escape by Night*, it was Ted Ray who received the guest starring credit.

A good example of the rivalry between father and son is the cover art of the program for the November 26, 1950 Annual Ball of the Grand Order of Water Rats. It features a cartoon of Andrew pushing father off the page, with the comment, "Make Way for the Young 'Uns, Old Timer."

At the age of thirteen, Andrew was signed to play the lead in the BBC Radio production of *Just William*, while his brother, Robin, age eighteen was signed to star in a Saturday morning show, *Hello There!* "Ted and I are still a bit bewildered by it all," said their mother. "We didn't say a word to the BBC — well, we didn't think they were that good, you know. Both the boys were sent for separately to be auditioned. And they were booked separately."[12]

Following *Escape by Night*, Andrew was a neglected son in *Escapade* (1955), with fourth billing after John Mills, Yvonne Mitchell and Alastair Sim; *A Prize of Gold* (1955), which had Andrew Ray's credit slipping down the cast list, way lower than stars Richard Widmark and Mai Zetterling; and was reunited with J. Lee Thompson for *Woman in a Dressing Gown*, in which he received slightly better billing.

He suddenly seemed to grow up into a very gangly and awkward young man with *Gideon's Day*, released in the U.S. as *Gideon of Scotland Yard* (1959), with Jack Hawkins in the title role. Andrew Ray plays a young police officer who gives chief inspector Gideon a ticket for going through a red light and begins a romantic relationship with Gideon's daughter, played by Anna Massey. He is still big enough a star that he is featured, with screen credit, in the trailer for the film.

After *Gideon's Day*, Andrew Ray returned to a more juvenile role in *The Young and the Guilty* (1959), as the son of Phyllis Calvert and Edward Chapman. In *Serious Charge*, released in the U.S. as *A Touch of a Hell* (1959), he is a nineteen-year-old petty criminal who accuses the local vicar, played by Anthony Quayle, of "interfering" with him. "Mr. Andrew Ray makes the boy a little too nasty," commented *The Times* (May 18, 1959). The film is perhaps most notable for having pop star Cliff Richard as the brother of the Andrew Ray character.

Andrew Ray had become a fairly regular actor on BBC and commercial television since the mid-1950s and had also appeared frequently in the West End in such plays as *I Capture the Castle* (Aldwych Theatre, March 1954), *Ring for Catty* (Lyric Theatre, February 1956) and *Less Than Kind* (Arts Theatre, June 1957).

He made only one film in the 1960s, *The Girl Getters* (1964), as a young man looking for sexual adventure in a seaside resort. No films in the 1970s, and two final films in the 1980s: a small role in the Burt Reynolds vehicle *Rough Cut* (1980) and an even smaller role in Charlotte Rampling's *Paris by Night* (1988), directed and written by David Hare.

Andrew Ray began his career playing cockney kids, but he became more aristocratic in his roles with the passing years. He was the Duke of York (later to be George VI) in *Crown Matrimonial*, which opened at the Theatre Royal, Haymarket, on October 19th, 1972, with Wendy Hiller as Queen Mary. He was again the Duke of York in the 1978 Thames Television mini-series, *Edward & Mrs. Simpson*, with Edward Fox and Cynthia Harris in the title roles. In the 1989 American television movie about Sir Harry Oakes, *Passion and Paradise* (1989), he was cast as the Duke of Windsor, a relatively small role, and again he played the Duke of Windsor in the travelogue, *Peter Ustinov on the Orient Express* (1991).

Andrew Ray's professional career ended in 1995 after five appearances as Dr. John Reginald in the Central Television production of *Peak Practice*.

The actor's personal life was often far more dramatic than any of the productions in which he had appeared, with more than one episode involving his father.

The most prominent issue, and one that must remain unresolved, is whether Ted Ray is actually Andrew Ray's biological father. Certainly, while Robin Ray bears a distinctive resemblance to his father, Andrew Ray does not. As Andrew's son, Mark, has written, "Ted and Andrew Ray differed in fundamental ways. Andrew could be impulsive and lived on the edge,"[13] while "Ted did things by the book." The question of paternity had never been raised until Mark discovered some notes that Andrew Ray had typed shortly before his death.

In them, he talked of a holiday with his mother in the South of France (actually it would appear to have been Greece) when she "drops a bombshell." The bombshell is that his father was a man named Barry Kennedy and not Ted Ray. She later retracted the statement, but when she was close to death, she began calling out for Barry Kennedy, although at the time grandson Mark claims she was suffering from dementia.

Although Andrew Ray would joke about the matter in later years, he was so upset at the time that he left the holiday and returned to the U.K.

All that Andrew Ray knew of his supposed father was that when he was a boy, "a fair-haired, rakish figure with a twinkle in his eye approached him in the street one day and said, 'Give my regards to your mother.' He said his name was Barry Kennedy." Ted Ray also supposedly met Kennedy at a golf club and told him, "If I ever see you again, it won't be a day too soon."[14]

Barry Kennedy was a dancer, actor and choreographer. He has one West End credit, as choreographer on a "musical frolic" titled *Fig Leaves*, which opened at the Adelphi Theatre on February 16th, 1940, and ran for a mere thirteen performances. At the time Andrew was conceived Kennedy was living at 37 Panton Street in Soho. Barry Kennedy was born on August 22nd, 1896, and died in the North London suburb of Islington early in 1974.[15]

Obviously, we will never know the truth in regard to Barry Kennedy and Andrew Ray. Barry Cryer claimed in an interview with the *Daily Express* that Ted Ray's attitude towards Andrew suggested he did not care for the boy:

"I was always taken aback when I heard Ted Ray talking about his sons in public. He would praise Robin to the hilt but never Andrew. He always referred to him as 'the other.' It was sad."[16]

However, Ted Ray's autobiography is full of fond comments relating to Andrew, of looking into his eyes and seeing his own. All three men, Ted, Robin and Andrew had blue eyes. Robin and Andrew did discuss the issue, with the former assuring him that his paternity was irrelevant in that it was Ted Ray who loved and raised him.

Ted Ray certainly took care of Andrew's earnings, investing them wisely in a trust until the boy was seventeen. At that time, Andrew gained control of a trust containing some 5,000 pounds, which he spent on two sports cars which he promptly wrecked. "I thought, it's my money and I have a right to spend it."[17]

One issue on which Ted and Andrew quite definitely did not see eye to eye was Andrew's wish to marry his girlfriend, actress Susan Burnet. He was nineteen and Susan was twenty. Ted Ray thought the couple too young, but Sybil eventually talked him round to the idea. They eventually married some six months later in 1959. Ted Ray refused to attend the wedding, although his excuse at the time was that he was away filming. Susan Burnet was born in Southern Rhodesia (Zimbabwe) in November 1938, and had come to England to study at the London Academy of Music and Dramatic Art (LAMDA). The couple had met while both were appearing on stage in *Flowering Cherry*, which opened at the Theatre Royal, Haymarket, on November 21, 1957, and which subsequently moved to Broadway. (In 1960-1961, Andrew Ray was back on Broadway, starring in Shelagh Delaney's *A Taste of Honey*.)

Susan Burnet worked on screen and television, but when Andrew decided to renounce materialism, she left show business and moved with him to Suffolk and a return to nature. While touring with a play in India, Andrew took up meditation and became more seriously involved with illegal drugs. The couple grew apart but did not divorce. Susan moved back to Rhodesia and was an enthusiastic supporter of the country's independence in 1980. She returned to the U.K. in 1986, working as an operator for British Telecom, her show business career very much over. There were two children, Madeleine (born 1963) and Mark (born 1966).

The couple had been back and forth to Rhodesia a number of times prior to Susan's settling there permanently. Andrew Ray never lived there after his wife's return, but he visited whenever he could. (In 1967, he appeared on stage in South Africa.) Andrew Ray's time in Rhodesia was checkered as he spoke out against the treatment of the black majority, and after independence, he joined the Zanu-PF party.

In the 1960s, Andrew Ray faced a dubious future, and in April 1965, at the age of twenty-five he attempted suicide, taking a drugs overdose. Certainly the success of his childhood years was not to be repeated, but he slowly began to rebuild his career, taking on character roles. He also showed that he had not lost his sense of fun. While making *Edward & Mrs. Simpson*, he met the now overweight Jessie Matthews. When he discovered that her notepaper was embossed "Jessie Matthews OBE,' he amended the heading to "Jessie Matthews OBESE." The lady was not amused and apparently Andrew Ray had to hide from her in the gents toilet.

Like his father, Andrew was an enthusiastic supporter of Arsenal Football Club and of boxing. "I never miss a big fight," wrote Ted Ray, devoting five pages of his autobiography to the sport and also revealing that he himself had joined a boxing club, presumably as a very young man.[18] Andrew Ray not only attended boxing matches but also spoke at boxing dinners. "Andrew was a great authority on boxing and much respected," said his friend and boxing agent Paddy Byrne. "Everybody loved him and he was great fun to be with, He was really into living."[19]

Andrew's interest in boxing did not apparently involve physical partici-pation. A news story was published in the *Daily Mirror* (May 8, 1953) that while shopping with his mother, the young, fourteen-year-old boy was attacked by a group of other boys, who pinned him down, went through his pockets and stole a few shillings. "Poor kid, he looked a worse mess than when he played the waif in *The Mudlark*," said Mrs. Ray. "But he should have screamed for help. All he says is, 'Boys don't scream in a fight."

Andrew Ray had just returned from a cycling holiday in Brighton when he visited a literary agent to discuss a possible biography of the Ray family. He spoke nonstop for twenty minutes. As the agent began to respond she noticed his eyes were closed. "Are you OK?" she asked. There was no reply. Andrew Ray had died. It was August 30th, 2003.

After his death, a park bench in his name, with the inscription, "No time to say goodbye," was installed in Hove, where Andrew had lived for some time. In the fall of 2019 it mysteriously disappeared.

Wife Susan died on January 17th, 2010 of lung cancer. Until his death, she and Andrew Ray had seen each other almost every day and they had remained good friends.

1. Robert Cannell, "Those Ted Ray Boys Catch on Fast…"

2. IMDB entry on Andrew Ray.

3. Susan Ray e-mail to Anthony Slide, dated August 12, 2020.

4. Ibid, dated August 23, 2020.

5. Ibid, dated August 26, 2020.

6. Nigel Rees diary, Monday, November 20th, 1972.

7. Anthony Slide interview with Miriam Margolyes, September 5, 2020.

8. Mark Olden, e-mail to Anthony Slide, August 19, 2020.

9. Susan Stranks' father, Australian-born Alan Stranks, created one of the most famous of radio policemen, P.C. 49, starring Brian Reece. Alan Stranks died while on vacation in Barcelona in June 1959.

10. Watching a 1975 episode of *Face the Music* on YouTube, I am reminded of what a kinder, gentler age we once lived through, where television programming emphasized intelligence.

11. Ted Ray, *Raising the Laughs*, p. 165.

12. Robert Cannell, "Those Ted Ray Boys Catch on Fast…"

13. Mark Olden, "Andrew Ray."

14. Ibid.

15. I am so grateful to Janice Healey for her incredible research in locating Barry Kennedy.

16. Mark Olden, "Andrew Ray."

17. Tom Vallance, "Andrew Ray."

18. Ted Ray, *Raising the Laughs*, pp. 141-145.

19. Patrick Newley, "Andrew Ray."

CHAPTER NINE

The End

With the passing years, Dennis Norden noticed that Ted Ray became "more diffident." The family had downsized, around 1961, moving from the Southgate home to 30 Broad Walk, Winchmore Hill, Middlesex, an area of London known for its celebrity residents. The Southgate house was not sold immediately, and the two sons and their respective wives were allowed to stay there.

Alcoholism

There can be no question that as he grew older, Ted Ray began to have more and more of a problem with alcoholism.

"He's working under a handicap, he's sober," as Kenneth Williams once commented, with that delightfully waspish voice of his, on the third episode of *The Betty Witherspoon Show*. It was obviously both a sarcastic and loaded comment. Actress Miriam Margolyes, who worked on the show with both men comments, "He was a drinker. Less competent therefore after lunch." She adds that once he had a drink "he wasn't very focused. I suppose he was an alcoholic."[1]

There can be no question Ted Ray had always enjoyed a drink or two, but by the 1970s, and perhaps earlier, he was obviously becoming an alcoholic. "Drink is a problem," he is reported to have said. "It's too easy to hit the bottle if you work the clubs. That's the sort of state I was in when I had my accident. A lot of my friends had died — and that's what I wanted to do."[2]

On Saturday, April 19, 1975, Ted Ray was involved in a serious car crash in the North London suburb of Palmer's Green. The comedian had been drinking heavily at the Crews Hill Golf Club, in large part, it was claimed, because the green was wet and he was unable to play. When he left the club, he was obviously drunk, but was there also a more sinister aspect to what was about to happen. Did he contemplate suicide at that moment? He drove his car on the wrong side of the road, striking a vehicle coming in the opposite direction. He failed to stop, and hit another car which was waiting to turn, and pushed it for some fifty yards before finally driving on the sidewalk and hitting a lamp post at forty miles per hour. Ray was thrown through the windshield and knocked unconscious. Suffering leg (broken in two places), hip (smashed), rib and facial injuries, he was taken to North Middlesex Hospital. It was a spectacular crash, and, luckily, aside from the comedian himself, nobody was injured.

The comedian's attorney, Henry Hill, tried to make light of the incident, blaming it on the weather, and explaining,

"If the course had been dry, he would have played his round and gone on his way and nobody would have been any worse."

Ted Ray was found to have three times the legal limit of alcohol in his blood. And there was little sympathy from his wife who told the press, "He's too bloody old to drive." On November 3, 1975, under his real name, Charles Olden, he appeared before North London magistrates and was fined a total of 370 pounds, ordered to pay costs, and banned from driving for three years.

The crash and the circumstances surrounding it destroyed Ted Ray's image as Mr. Nice Guy.

Unfortunately, the comedian began to joke about the incident, in all probability in a desperate attempt to cover up the helplessness he felt regarding his career, It was not an approach which went over well with readers of the *Daily Mirror*. He told the newspaper (May 10, 1975):

"Quite frankly, I don't even know if I have a future. I don't even know that when I try to stand up I won't fall down. That would practically spell the end of stage appearances. Fortunately I had given them up. I suppose I could carry on doing my panel games on radio and television."

Basically, Ted Ray had lost the will to live. "I didn't care what happened to me," he was reported to have said, "I'd go to sleep at night just hoping I wouldn't wake up next day."[3]

He was both bitter and depressed, haunted by the realization that he might have injured or killed someone else. He continued on with *Does the Team Think?*, but that, basically, constituted his career from this point onwards. He might have tried for club bookings, but he hated the blue material that audience demanded, audiences who, as he pointed out, cared nothing for quick words unless some of them were dirty. There were reports that he was back in his stride again when, on October 24th, 1977, he was the unexpected star of a Variety Club luncheon tribute at the Savoy Hotel for Jimmy Jewel's fifty years in show business. The latter commented,

"Put a lunch in Ted's mouth and up comes a speech. Put a speech in my mouth and up comes a lunch."

The Times reviewer noted that while Ted Ray was walking with the aid of a stick, he needed no artificial aids to deliver his outrageous puns. He, Alfred Marks and Jon Pertwee "made after-dinner speeches that bore all the hallmarks of the hard old school that produced the best stand-up comedians."[4]

However, on Thursday, November 3rd, Ted Ray was admitted to hospital for what was claimed to be check on his hip operation. While in hospital he suffered a heart attack. The following Monday, wife Sybil visited him for the last time, and his parting words to her were "Don't forget I love you." "I think we both knew it was goodbye," she said. The comedian died at 4:00 a.m. on Tuesday, November 8th 1977.

"I am not a weepy woman and what matters is that we were married for 45 years and had a wonderful life."[5]

One is reminded of the story that Ted Ray awoke one morning and said, "Sybil…darling…I don't want you to be alarmed but I think I've had a heart attack. I'm paralyzed all down my arm." She replied, "You silly fool, you've been lying on it and got pins and needles." As her daughter-in-law Susan points out that pretty much sums up their whole approach to illness. "If you're sick, shut up and go to bed!"[6]

The *Daily Mail* (November 9, 1977) was anxious to define Ted Ray as the type of individual who identified with his audience:

"Ray was special because he was a professional's professional who told jokes at 250 words a minute yet still sold himself to audiences as one of their own."

Describing him as a pillar of traditional British entertainment, the *Daily Mail* continued, "Unlike most of his competition, Ted seemed to embody Mr. Ordinary."

The Times (November 9, 1977) described him as "a character who gave music hall modes a lease of life in an age of radio and television…Ted Ray belonged, above all else, to the music hall. He came to the stage when the music hall was already reaching an end, but preserved its manners and traditions throughout his career…His death puts a lovable and honoured tradition at risk."

Sybil refused to go to the funeral. "I have made up my mind not to cry," she said. "In a way it is better that he has gone and does not have to face any more pain." Grandson Mark recalls that "she was devastated by his death."[7] The funeral took place at the Golders Green Crematorium, and the body was cremated. What happened to his ashes is not known.

He left an estate worth 191,199 pounds, which is the equivalent today of 1,118,000.00 pounds. Not an incredibly large amount considering Ted Ray's fame and habit of working practically non-stop.

Grandson Mark Olden writes,

"It might seem strange to say in light of Barry Kennedy and the paternity question, but I should reiterate that Sybil was devoted to Ted. I spent a lot of time with her up to her death in 2002, and barely a day went by when she didn't mention him, his pictures were everywhere, etc., and my dad told me how she was incredibly supportive of his career. Relationships can be complex, and Sybil was no exception."[8] It might well have been grief that prevented Sybil's visiting with her husband at the end.

1. Anthony Slide, interview with Miriam Margolyes, September 5, 2020.

2. "A Comedian and Former Red Dies."

3. Ibid.

4. "The Serious Side of Being Funny," p. 12. The commentator pointed out that in contrast a rambling speech by a newcomer, Tom O'Connor raised scarcely a titter. He happens to be the author of *Tom O'Connor's Book of Liverpool Humour* (1987).

5. Michael Owen, "Ted Ray, the King of the Wisecrack Is dead," p.3.

6. Susan Ray, e-mail to Anthony Slide, August 12, 2020.

7. Mark Olden, e-mail to Anthony Slide, August 31, 2020.

8. Ibid.

CHAPTER TEN

Heritage

Ted Ray began his career at the tail end of the music hall era, and it was an era with which he was fascinated and which he appreciated. An argument might well be made that as a stand-up comic he kept that era alive. And for that we should be grateful. Certainly, the comedian never forgot those who had come before him, and he fully embraced the legacy of the legends of the music hall.

In his autobiography, he wrote of appearing at the famous old music hall, the Canterbury, on Waterloo Bridge Road, with the knowledge that when a comedian got to the punch line, a train would rumble by overhead and the joke be destroyed. But, it was here that such legends of the music hall as Marie Lloyd, Dan Leno, Eugene Stratton, and Albert Chevalier had appeared. Marie Lloyd's sister, Rosie, seemed at times to be a regular on the bill with Ted Ray.

On the final episode of the fourth season of *The Ted Ray Show*, televised on May 10th, 1958, he appeared with Joan Turner in a tribute to George Robey and Violet Lorraine, singing, "If You Were the Only Girl in the World."

Ted Ray was a big fan of Birmingham-born Sid Field, who carried on the music hall tradition after World War Two and who died at an early age in February 1950. Ted Ray was there, along with Laurence Olivier, to read the lesson at a memorial service at St. Martin-in-the-Field.

Ted Ray also wrote of the unique character of music hall audiences, with their "unerring instinct for what is good and what is sincere." Those audiences and audiences that followed recognized those qualities in Ted Ray's work.

But, with the passing of time, there was a generational gap between stand-up comedy, as represented by Ted Ray, and stand-up comedy from later performers who might be able to retain a memory for jokes, but a memory for jokes that were unrestrained in their references to sexual and scatological matters. The early performers of British Music Hall were lucky in having Ted Ray to remember and honor them. There was no such remembrance for Ted Ray. He was, and remains largely forgotten.

Today's best British comedians show a forceful side to their comedy. They will get their points of view, their humor, across with determination and often with outrage. Ted Ray was relatively low key in comparison, say, to Lee Mack or David Mitchell. Jo Brand is more gentle and closer in quality to Ted Ray than her male counterparts.

On *The Betty Witherspoon Show*, Kenneth Williams sang "Everyone 's Got Nostalgia Madness." Sadly, not for Ted Ray's style of comedy

"He was a widely talented man," wrote Michael Dynan in *The Stage*, "but I suspect that it was these same qualities which contributed to the fact that we hear so little about him nowadays. It is all too easy to better remember artists who were known mainly for just a few excellent comedy routines, rather than those with a much broader talent, such as Ted Ray."

In *Untold Stories*, based on his diaries, Alan Bennett hails Ted Ray as "a cheeky chappie," along with Arthur Askey, Dickie Henderson, Tommy Trinder, and Max Miller. A strange group in a way, as Ted Ray is so unlike the other representatives of cheeky chappiehood. What links them, as Alan Bennett notes is that the represent a non-London specific type of comedy:

"A child of the north, I don't care for cockneys or their much-advertised Blitz-defeating cheerfulness: all that knees-up, thumbs in the lapels down at the old Bull and Bush cockney sparrerdom has always left me cold."[1]

Writing on his website in tribute to Ken Dodd, Ian McKellen noted,

"Many of the comedians of my youth were from Liverpool; I heard them on radio. Tommy Handley in wartime *ITMA* was the most celebrated, though I preferred Ted Ray in *Ray's a Laugh.* [2]

When Ken Dodd died, many of the obituaries made reference to Ted Ray and Arthur Askey as Dodd's contemporaries although, of course, they both pre-dated him. Asked, on one of his television specials, about his fellow comedians, Ken Dodd commented off the cuff,

"The greatest stand-up comic of them all was Ted Ray. A wonderful man. He had such charm, such sophistication."[3]

---

1. Alan Bennett, *Untold Stories*, pp. 417-418.

2. Quoted in *Liverpool Echo*, https//www.liverpoolecho.co.uk (accessed August 2020).

3. *An Audience with Ken Dodd*, London Weekend Television, December 3, 1994.

Stand-Up Comedy: A Brief History

It is not outrageous to claim that Ted Ray was perhaps the greatest stand-up comedian of the 20th Century. Only Arthur Askey and Ken Dodd can be mentioned in the same breath. There are others, of course, who should not be ignored, most notably Morecambe and Wise, Jimmy Jewel and Ben Warriss, Jimmy Wheeler, Max Miller, Tommy Trinder (described as one of Britain's best ad-lib comedians), and Frank Randle.[1] In tribute to Ted Ray's fame, and standing (no pun intended) in the genre, it seems appropriate to add an appendix discussing the history of stand-up comedy — obvious as it might appear to be.

According to the *Oxford English Dictionary*, stand-up comic is a term first used in the mid-1960s. Obviously, while a stand-up comic may not have been defined as such prior to the 1960s, both in Britain and the United States, he dates back to another century. It should be noted that stand-up comics do not need to deliver their acts from a standing position. At the end of his life, following his car crash, Ted Ray performed seated on a stool. Around this same time, another stand-up comic, Dave Allen, would perform seated with a glass of whiskey and a cigarette.

In the United Kingdom, stand-up comedy can be traced back to the 1840s, when comedians and singers of comic songs appeared in supper clubs. Within less than a decade, the music hall had become established, and a primary focus of the bill was the stand-up comic. He would not perhaps be recognizable to audiences familiar with stand-up comics of today. The emphasis was not so much on jokes but more on comic monologues, and the master of the craft was Dan Leno (1860-1904), who became one of the highest-paid comedians in the world, with his discussion of Mrs. Kelly: "Oh, you must know Mrs. Kelly; everybody knows Mrs. Kelly." When he appeared in the United States, he was billed as "The Funniest Man in the World."

Just as vocalists needed to develop a special technique in order that their voices might be heard throughout an auditorium, so did stand-up comics have to rely on the strength of their voices to get across their acts. Dan Leno was fairly diminutive in size, but he experienced no recorded difficulty in projecting his voice not only on the music hall stage but also in pantomimes at the Theatre Royal, Drury Lane. The exact date is not known, but by the 1930s, stand-up comics certainly had the use of microphones — not one they held in their hand, but rather one behind which they stood. The microphone on stage had its origins in the microphone of the recording studios and the microphone of the radio broadcasters dating back a decade or more.

The Theatres Act of 1843 by which the Lord Chamberlain's Office approved and censored all theatrical work, referenced only a "stage play," but as part of an addendum, these two words were taken to include "every tragedy, comedy, farce, opera, burletta [a brief comic opera], interlude, melodrama, pantomime, or other entertainment of the stage or any part thereof." In other words, it was applied in theory to stand-up comedians and, of course, pantomimes.

The comedians were initially to be found in saloons and pubs, but gradually, in the 1800s, the music hall was developed. Its content, indeed its existence, was approved and determined by local councils and both local magistrates, whose initial concerns appear to have been the use of the music halls by prostitutes plying their trade rather than what was taking place on stage. Indeed, it seems difficult to censor performances based on scripts or song lyrics in that the presentation was in the gestures used by the performer. A song by Marie Lloyd, for example, might seem relatively harmless but when she added gestures to the lyrics, the meaning became more lurid and questionable.

Eventually, it was up to the owners or managers of the music halls to "censor" what was acceptable. At the end of the 19th Century, Oswald Stoll and Edward Moss controlled almost forty variety theatres in the United Kingdom, and comedians appearing in their variety houses or music halls were careful not to offend the sensibilities of the two gentlemen.

The Lord Chamberlain was responsible for what was performed on stage, but that was not his primary function — he was more concerned with royal protocol, state visits, the state opening of parliament, and other major events involving the monarch. He realized that it was virtually impossible to censor what took place on the music hall stage. There was simply too much ad-libbing. The music hall was considered working class entertainment, and more important to the Lord Chamberlain was what was presented to middle class audiences at legitimate theatres. As

Professor Stephen J. Nicholson, an authority on British stage censorship points out,

"There were all sorts of complicating issues. At one time there were debates in the Lord Chamberlain's office (and beyond) about what was the difference between a sketch and a play (because the former were not subject to the Lord Chamberlain). Some argued that a series of songs punctuated by dialogue should count as a play. Because music halls as venues were treated as exempt, some writers (including George Bernard Shaw) had one-act plays staged there in order to avoid submitting them to the Lord Chamberlain. To confuse things further, revues staged in theatres (e.g. the Windmill) were treated as plays and required a license from the Lord Chamberlain."[2]

Because of this, some comedians found that they could not perform the same gags in theatres as they had performed in music halls. The most famous example is Frank Randle (1901-1957), whose truly awful comedy has been defended by some as surreal, and, therefore, difficult for modern audiences to acknowledge. "The master of the single entendre," as Frank Randle was known appeared in the pantomime of *Mother Goose* (and pantomimes did come under the Lord Chamberlain's purview). The Lord Chamberlain had his performance watched by the police every night for a week, and would demand the deletion of various lines and gestures. No wonder that Frank Randle billed himself as "Star of Stage, Screen and Magistrate's Court."

(As an aside, in the 1930s, the Lord Chamberlain did not permit criticism or mockery of Hitler or the Nazis, and in 1935, one comedian in the pantomime *Robinson Crusoe* was prosecuted and fined for including a physical impersonation of Hitler which had not appeared in the script submitted to the Lord Chamberlain's Office.)

While comedians could ad-lib with impunity on the music hall stage, this was not true in the legitimate theatre. In the 1960s, the Royal Court Theatre in London presented a play which involved actors responding to questions from the audience. The Lord Chamberlain would only permit this if all the questions and answers were submitted to him in advance.

Stephen J. Nicholson points out that,

"You have to remember that quite a lot of the time the Lord Chamberlain was probably happy to turn a blind eye to some of what happened — so long as it wasn't exposed by the press and he didn't get criticised too much for what he had allowed. There were various occasions when particular newspapers launched campaigns against 'filth' and decadence in both theatres and music halls — and the Lord Chamberlain almost invariably felt bound to respond and cover his back by making sure he was seen to be tough."[3]

All comedians appearing on the legitimate stage or in revue were required to submit a script of their acts to the Lord Chamberlain's Office. After reading, the script was returned with unacceptable jokes underlined in blue pencil. Thus, it is believed "blue" became used to define comedians who specialized in "dirty" jokes as part of their act. (There are other explanations as to the use of the word "blue".)

One of the most famous of the blue comedians was Max Miller (1894-1963), "the cheeky chappie," whom many would argue was the greatest stand-up comedian of his generation. He was known for his flamboyant and totally vulgar attire and his risqué jokes which relied on the double entendre. His catch phrases included "Now, there's a funny thing" and "It's people like you who give me a bad name." A typical joke might be "Have you heard about the girl of eighteen who swallowed a pin, but didn't feel the prick until she was twenty-one."

In 1944, he was invited to Windsor Castle to give a special private performance for King George VI and Queen Elizabeth. The Lord Chamberlain asked that this information not be leaked to the press as it had the potential to cause him embarrassment and make it harder to censor Miller in the future.

With the advent of World War Two, stand-up comedians found themselves "drafted" to entertain the troops through ENSA (Entertainments National Service Association). There was no censorship of routines performed for the troops, and because of the situation, comedians felt able to introduce a considerable amount of what might be described as obscenity into their gags. "A beautiful excuse for smut," as it was defined. In January 1940, the *Sunday Dispatch* complained,

"'Broader and bluer' seems to be the slogan of entertainment these days and nights. A rash of rudery-crudery has broken out since the war started, and jokes called the 'doubtful' kind are being heard in unusual places from unexpected lips."

These "unusual places" included not only makeshift theatres for troop entertainment, but also the BBC, where standards were relaxed as part of the war effort. The *Sunday Dispatch* reported, "The most surprising relaxation in censorship has been that of the BBC…There seems to be very little supervision now, and the comedians are slipping in a surprising number of hot ones."

The Lord Chamberlain's Office had no responsibility for what was presented either by ENSA or the BBC, but it did find it necessary to go on the defensive, noting that comedians were adding gags which were not in approved scripts. Comedians argued that topical and improvised gags were crucial to their routines — and, after all, what were they fighting for?

Vic Oliver (1898-1964), a Jewish comedian, is best remembered for his marriage to Winston Churchill's daughter, a marriage of which the prime minister did not approve. Churchill proved himself to be the equal of many stand-up comics when he was asked whom he admired most and responded, "Mussolini. Because he had the good sense to shoot his son-in-law."

The comedian wrote in 1939 to the Lord Chamberlain,

"I have been informed by the producer of our show *Black Velvet* currently running at the London Hippodrome that in future no new jokes or bits of business or any spontaneous remarks must be made, without first obtaining permission from the Lord Chamberlain's Office.

"I do hope in the interests of the top-line comedians, as well as the young, aspiring comedians, that you will be gracious enough to modify this ruling as otherwise our profession will receive a serious setback, and the inventing of any jokes and witty remarks will have to become a thing of the past. As you know, spontaneity is the basis of every joke, and the biggest laughs of all are produced from topical patter."[4]

Vic Oliver suggested that comedians be allowed to tell a joke once, and then submit it to the Lord Chamberlain's Office. The latter remained firm. There could be no compromise. The law was the law.

The role of the Lord Chamberlain as theatre censor was abolished with the passing of the Theatres Act of 1968.

Of course today, comedians are self-censoring thanks to "cancel culture" and "wokeness". However, while comedians who specialize in stand-up comedy are strong in their opposition to what they perceive as the destruction of comedy as we know it, it has been pointed out that the more offensive a comedy routine, the more it would seem to appeal to those in a position of authority. *The Guardian* (August 10, 2021) commented that on his 2019 tour, Jimmy Carr was still making jokes about dwarfism, lesbians and gypsies, while the BBC was steadily signing him for prominent TV gigs. *The Guardian* continued, "The idea that cancel culture is killing comedy is a nonsense slogan — an absurdist joke in itself."

In Ted Ray's era, stand-up comedians were white and male. The first black stand-up comedian to become well-known was Charlie Williams (1927-2006), who enjoyed an earlier career after World War Two as one of Britain's first Black footballers. In 1971, he was featured on Granada

Television's *The Comedians*, and the following year, he enjoyed a season at the London Palladium.

Charlie Williams was born in Yorkshire, and had a catch-phrase, "me old flower," which seemed appropriate for his background and for his Yorkshire accent. "Me mother's from Yorkshire. My father is anyone's guess." He was very much of his time, when the BBC was presenting *The Black and White Minstrel Show*, and when a black entertainer such as Williams was expected to tell jokes against himself. Audiences expected him to ridicule the color of his skin with comments such as "I'm perspiring a lot, I'm leaking chocolate." "Don't rub your eyes, love. With all that mascara, you'll be darker than me," he would tell a female audience member.

He was totally ambivalent as to the color of his skin. Williams saw nothing wrong in making reference to "Pakis" in his jokes. Racist politician Enoch Powell was the subject of many jokes, but never, incredibly, in a negative way. When his father came over from the West Indies after World War One, Britishers accepted him because he was one of only a small number. Today, as Charlie Williams, pointed out too many were headed to the U.K., and it was understandable that there should be a racist response. Quite extraordinary. But then, as he once explained, "I don't have any regrets…I told jokes that I thought would suit the audience."

Of course, even today, there are remarkably few Black comedians on the British stage, with the only one with any major reputation being Lenny Henry.[5] Of Charlie Williams, he has commented,

"I would go to see Charlie pulling the house down doing stuff about 'darkies' and I thought this is obviously what you've got to do if it's a predominantly white audience — you've got to put yourself, and other people, down."

Gay comedians did not flourish during much of Ted Ray's career for the obvious reason that homosexuality was a crime until 1967. In the 1950s, Larry Grayson (1923-1995) began his career as a "camp" comedian, certainly limp-wristed, although he did not reference his homosexuality. Grayson would use the catch phrase of "Shut that door". But, in reality, he opened the door for the gay comedians who followed him. Preceding Larry Grayson was Frankie Howerd (1917-1992), whose career began with his entertaining troops during World War Two, and who tried, one might almost claim foolishly, to hide his homosexuality.

Ironically, the Lord Chamberlain's Office would not permit any serious discussion of homosexuality on stage, while it found no issue with the treatment of homosexuality in a comic fashion. Effeminate, comic gay men crop up fairly commonly in British films of the 1930s and 1940s.

Even Frank Randle has a hulking and threatening male appear effeminate when talking and walking in his 1949 short comedy, *Bella's Birthday*. These are the sort of gay men that John Inman would impersonate, although he himself, while certainly gay, cannot be categorized as a stand-up comic but rather a comic actor.

There are no famous female stand-up comics from the Ted Ray era. Indeed, it might be argued that the only three comediennes from the era with any lasting fame are Cicely Courtneidge, Gracie Fields and Thora Hird. Despite their considerable talent, no member of that trio can truly be identified as a stand-up comic. Perhaps closest to a genuine female stand-up comic is Hylda Baker (1905-1986), who would gossip on stage with her mute stooge, played by a tall male in female attire. "She knows, y'know," Hylda would assure the audience.

With typical brilliance, Alan Bennett describes Hylda Baker as "common, hilariously so, over-dressed, under-educated and unashamed of it, both on stage and off, pictured once in the *Evening Post* driving through Leeds in an open limousine with a monkey on a gold chain and a fetching young chauffeur in much the same position."

It should be noted that there were certainly female performers in the 1800s who billed themselves as "comics" or serio-comics," for example Florrie Gallimore. But, in reality, she would change the mood of her audience from sadness to laughter with her songs, and appeared as a male impersonator.

Obviously, some stand-up comics did not need to change their acts from one year to another, while others thrived on the topicality of their routines. Some gags went out of fashion, for example those relating to mothers-in-law, while other remained popular for decade, such as those relating to homosexuality and foreigners, particularly those of color.

With the advent of television, stand-up comedians from the music hall found a new and lucrative outlet. They didn't actually finesse their acts, but rather repeated what had appealed to theatre audiences. And the BBC had *The Good Old Days*, which supposedly recreated the golden era of the music hall, encouraging the audience to resort to fancy dress as it roared approval at a master of ceremonies and laughed uproariously at comedy routines that were long past their prime. As has been pointed out, Arthur Askey, for example, would simply appear, say "Hello Playmates," and then sing a song about a busy, busy bee. Seems unfunny? Well, as John Mooney in his "Slugger O'Toole" blogsite has pointed out, it was better in black-and-white. From television variety shows, it was only a short step to panel games, on which comedians seem interchangeable from week to week.

Again to quote John Mooney, these first stand-up comedians on television represented the establishment, resolutely conservative in outlook. Mooney continues,

"Now of course, there is a new Establishment. Not necessarily lefties, Not necessarily liberals. But certainly London-centric elite. I mean those old variety/music hall types might have been to the political right of Atilla the Hun but at least they knew where Grimsby, Middlesbrough and Stoke-on-Trent were. And maybe they had more respect for the ordinary working people up there than any of the anti-Brexit funny men and funny women on BBC."

One of the largest audiences before whom Ted Ray appeared comprised some 8,000 members of a businessmen's organization called Round Tables in Britain and Ireland (R.T.B.I.). It took place in the ballroom of the Butlin's Holiday Camp in Pwllheli, Wales. Ted Ray was quite rightly nervous, suspecting he would "die on his arse." In fact, he went on stage and did a stand-up comedy routine lasting one hour. As he left the stage, he asked the host if he could go back and do more — and then proceeded to do another thirty minutes of comedy.[6]

In a way stand-up comedians have come full circle, from appearing at drinking and supper clubs in the mid-1800s to appearing at working mens' clubs in the 1970s and later. Catering to working class men — women were not invited to join until the early 21st Century — the concept of a working man's club is almost as old as the notion of supper clubs. They were intended to provide education for the working classes and to lure them away from the pubs. Ultimately, the working mens' clubs became an outlet for cheap alcohol, combined with cheap entertainment.

The stand-up comic was a staple of these clubs, earning on average around forty pounds a show in the 1970s to 200 pounds or more in the 21st Century. The working mens' clubs were the equivalent of the American borscht belt, a training ground for new, young comedians, and a retirement home for comedians edging towards the end of their careers. The emphasis was almost constantly on offensive humor and profanity. Political correctness did not exist. Among the better known stand-up comedians of the 1970s who enjoyed fame thanks to the clubs are Roy Chubby Brown, Frank Carson, Jim Davidson, Les Dawson, Peter Kay, and Bernard Manning.

Roy Chubby Brown had success with a song titled "Living Next Door to Alice (Who the Fuck Is Alice?)" Jim Davidson has become noted in recent years for his adult pantomimes, with songs such as "I Have to Start Wanking Again". He refused to perform when he found the front row of the audience was taken up with people in wheelchairs, and has been described as "extraordinarily foul-mouthed, racist, and sexist." Bernard Manning denied ever using the word "wog," but found nothing wrong with using "nigger" and "coon".

Obviously, what is said in working mens' clubs should remain in working mens' clubs.

If nothing else, the routines of this working mens' clubs breed of comedians make one realize just how superior were their predecessors, such as Ted Ray, Arthur Askey and Ken Dodd, who might occasionally tell a risqué joke but never set out to offend any minority group. As Ken Dodd would say, "I'm not homophobic. I've never been bitten by a dog."

1. I am ignoring some comedians, such as Flanagan and Allen, Robb Wilton and George Formby, in that their performances were not limited to stand-up comedy, but also included sketches or musical numbers.

2. Stephen J. Nicholson, e-mail to Anthony Slide, November 8, 2021.

3. Ibid.

4. Stephen J. Nicholson, follow-up e-mail to Anthony Slide, November 8, 2021.

5. I am not including the brilliant Richard Ayoade as a stand-up comic. While he qualifies as a black comedian, he is actually the son of a Norwegian mother.

6. Information from Bryn Williams, *Red Tails in the Sunset*.

Ted Ray Filmography

Ideal Cine Magazine No. 357. Released 1933. 10 MINUTES.

Radio Parade of 1935. Wardour/British International Pictures. Released December 1934. DIRECTOR: Arthur Woods. SCREENPLAY: Jack Davies, Paul Perez, James Bunting, and Arthur Woods, based on a story by Reginald Purdell and John Watt. With Will Hay, Helen Chandler, Clifford Mollison, Davy Burnaby, and Lily Morris. As Himself. 96 MINUTES. Released in the U.S. as *Radio Follies.*

Pathe Gazette No. 11/Dig for Victory. Released 1943. 10 MINUTES.

A Ray of Sunshine. Adelphi. Released August 1950. DIRECTOR: Horace Shepard. With Wilson, Keppel & Betty, Janet Brown, Morton Frazer's Harmonica Gang, and Ivy Benson and Her Girls Band. As Himself. 55 MINUTES.

Meet Me Tonight. British Film Makers/General Film Distributors. Released September 1952. DIRECTOR: Anthony Pelissier. SCREENPLAY: Noel Coward, based on his play *Tonight at 8:30 (Red Peppers).* With Kay Walsh, Martita Hunt, Frank Pettingell, and Bill Fraser. As George Pepper. 85 MINUTES. Released in the U.S. as *Tonight at 8:30.*

Escape by Night. Tempean/Eros. Released January 1954. DIRECTOR AND SCREENPLAY: John Gilling. With Bonar Colleano, Andrew Ray, Sidney James, Simone Silva, and Patrick Barr. As Mr. Weston. 79 MINUTES.

My Wife's Family. Forth Films/Associated British Pictures. Released November 1956. DIRECTOR: Gilbert Gunn. SCREENPLAY: Gilbert Gunn and Talbot Rothwell, based on the play by Fred Duprez. With Ronald Shiner, Greta Gynt, Robertson Hare, Fabia Drake, and Diane Hart. As Jack Gay. 76 MINUTES.

The Crowning Touch. Crescent/Butcher's Film Service. Released June 1959. DIRECTOR: David Eady. SCREENPLAY: Margot Bennett, based on a story by Cecily Finn and Joan O'Connor. With Greta Gynt, Griffith Jones, Sydney Taffler, Dermot Walsh, and Irene Handle. As Bert. 75 MINUTES.

Carry on Teacher. Beaconsfield/Anglo-Amalgamated. Released August 1959. DIRECTOR: Gerald Thomas. SCREENPLAY: Norman Hudis. With Kenneth Connor, Charles Hawtrey, Leslie Phillips, Joan Sims, and Kenneth Williams. As William Wakefield. 86 MINUTES.

Please Turn Over. Beaconsfield/Anglo-Amalgamated. Released December 1959. DIRECTOR: Gerald Thomas. SCREENPLAY: Norman Hudis, based on a play by Basil Thomas. With Jean Kent, Leslie Phillips, Joan Sims, Julia Lockwood, Charles Hawtrey, and Dilys Laye. As Ernest Halliday. 87 MINUTES.

Andrew Ray Filmography

The Mudlark. 20th Century-Fox. Released November 1950. DIRECTOR: Jean Negulesco. SCREENPLAY: Nunnally Johnson, based on the novel by Theodore Bonnet. With Irene Dunne, Alec Guinness, Beatrice Campbell, Finlay Currie, Anthony Steel, Raymond Lovell, and Edward Rigby. As Wheeler. 100 MINUTES.

The Yellow Balloon. Marble Arch/Associated British Pictures Corporation. Released December 1952. DIRECTOR: J. Lee Thompson. SCREENPLAY: J. Lee Thompson and Ann Burnaby, based on a story by Ann Burnaby. With William Sylvester, Kenneth More, Kathleen Ryan, Bernard Lee, Hy Hazell, and Marjorie Rhodes. As Frankie. 80 MINUTES.

Escape by Night. Tempean/Eros. Released January 1954. Director and SCREENPLAY: John Gilling. With Bonar Colleano, Sidney James, Simone Silva, and Patrick Barr. As Joey Weston. 79 MINUTES.

A Prize of Gold. Warwick/Columbia Pictures. Released February 1955. DIRECTOR: Mark Robson. SCREENPLAY: Robert Buckner and John Paxton, based on a novel by Max Catto. With Richard Widmark, Mai Zetterling, Nigel Patrick, George Cole, Donald Wolfit, Joseph Tomelty, and Eric Pohlmann. As Conrad. 100 MINUTES. Reissued 1961.

Escapade. Pinnacle/Eros. Released July 1955. DIRECTOR: Philip Leacock. SCREENPLAY: Gilbert Holland, based on a play by Roger Macdougall. With John Mills, Yvonne Mitchell, Alastair Sim, Jeremy Spencer, Marie Lohr, and Peter Asher. As Max Hampden. 87 MINUTES.

Woman in a Dressing Gown. Godwin-Willis/Associated British Pictures Corporation. Released October 1957. DIRECTOR: J. Lee Thompson. SCREENPLAY: Ted Willis, based on his television play. With Yvonne Mitchell, Sylvia Sims, Anthony Quayle, Carole Leslie, Olga Lindo, and Harry Locke. As Brian Preston. 94 MINUTES.

Gideon's Day. Columbia British Pictures. Released March 1958. DIRECTOR: John Ford. SCREENPLAY: T.E.B. Clarke, based on the novel by J.J. Maric. With Jack Hawkins, Dianne Foster, Cyril Cusack, James Hayter, Ronald Howard, Anna Massey, and Anna Lee. As Simon Farnaby-Green. 91 MINUTES. Released in the U.S. as *Gideon of Scotland Yard.*

The Young and the Guilty. Welwyn/Associated British Pictures Corporation. Released March 1958. DIRECTOR: Peter Cotes. SCREENPLAY: Ted Willis, based on his television play. With Phyllis Calvert, Edward Chapman, Janet Munro, Campbell Singer, and Hilda Fenemore. As Eddie Marshall. 67 MINUTES.

Serious Charge. Alva/Eros. Released April 1959. DIRECTOR: Terence Young. SCREENPLAY: Mickey Delamar and Guy Elmes, based on a play by Philip King. With Anthony Quayle, Sarah Churchill, Cliff Richard, Liliane Brousse, Irene Brown, Wilfred Pickles, and Percy Herbert. As Larry Thompson. 99 MINUTES.

Twice round the Daffodils. GWH Productions. Released February 1962. DIRECTOR: Gerald Thomas. SCREENPLAY: Norman Hudis, based on the play, *Ring for Catty,* by Patrick Cargill and Jack Beale. With Juliet Mills, Donald Sinden, Donald Houston, Kenneth Williams, Ronald Lewis, and Joan Sims. As Chris Walker. 89 MINUTES.

The System. Kenneth Shipman/Bryanston Films. Released February 1964. DIRECTOR: Michael Winner. SCREENPLAY: Peter Draper. With Oliver Reed, Jane Merrow, Barbara Ferris, Harry Andrews, Julia Foster, John Alderton, and Ann Lynn. As Willy. 90 MINUTES. Released in the U.S. as *The Girl Getters.*

Rough Cut. David Merrick Productions/Paramount Pictures. Released June 1980. DIRECTOR: Don Siegel. SCREENPLAY: Francis Burns (Larry Gelbart), based on a novel by Derek Lambert. With Burt Reynolds, Lesley-Anne Down, David Niven, Timothy West, Patrick Magee, and Josh Ackland. As Pilbrow. 112 MINUTES.

Paris by Night. British Screen Productions. Released April 1989. DIRECTOR AND SCREENPLAY: David Hare. With Charlotte Rampling, Michael Gambon, Iain Glen, Robert Morley, Jane Asher, and Niamh Cusack. As Michael Swanton. 103 MINUTES.

Anderson, Robert, "Being Funny Is a Serious Business," *Aberdeen Evening Express*, March 15, 1957, p. 4.

Ashworth, Margaret, "Lost BBC: *Ray's a Laugh*," *The Conservative Woman*, June 9, 2019, *https://conservativewoman.co.uk*.

Barfe, Louis. *Turned Out Nice Again: The Story of British Home Entertainment*. London: Atlantic Books, 2008.

______. *Happiness and Tears: The Ken Dodd Story*. London: Apollo Books, 2019.

Barker, Dennis, "Andrew Ray," *The Guardian*, August 26, 2003, *https://www.theguardian.com/news/2003/aug/26/guardianobituaries.film* (accessed August 2020).

Bennett, Alan. *Untold Stories*. London: Faber and Faber, 2005.

"The Boy Bibi: Andrew Ray on His London Debut," *The Stage*, February 11, 1952, p. 11.

"Busy Time for Ted Ray," *Birmingham Daily Post*, September 27, 1958, p. 17.

Cannell, Robert, "Those Ted Ray Boys Catch on Fast…," source unknown.

Chester, Charlie. *The World Is Full of Charlies*. London: New English Library, 1974.

Coady, Matthew, "The Man Who Survived Vaudeville," *Daily Mirror*, November 27, 1968.

"A Comedian and Former Red Dies," *https://playupliverpool.com/1977/11/08* (accessed August 2020).

"Comedy and Personality: Ted Ray on Building an Act," *The Stage*, September 13, 1951, pp. 1, 5.

Dibbs, Martin. *Radio Fun and the BBC Variety Department, 1922-67*. London: Palgrave Macmillan, 2019.

Dynan, Michael, "Late, Great, Funny Man," *The Stage*, November 6, 1997, p. 11.

Edwards, Bob, "Meet the Comic Pioneers Who Made Liverpool the Funny Factory of Britain, *Good News*, February 26, 2016, *https://www.goodnewsliverpool.co.uk* (accessed August 2020).

Fletcher, Cyril. *Nice One Cyril*. London: Barrie & Jenkins, 1978.

Forrest, Elizabeth, "Threesome," *Picturegoer*, October 4, 1952, pp. 19, 26.

Gifford, Denis. *The Golden Age of Radio*. London: London: B.T. Batsford, 1985.

______, "Obituary: Robin Ray," *The Independent*, November 30, 1998, *https://www.independent.co.uk/arts-entertainment/obituary-robinray* (accessed July 2020).

Gray, Andy, "Ted Ray," *The Stage and Television Today*, November 17, 1977, p. 6.

Hirst, Robert, "Ted Ray Looks Back," *Liverpool Echo*, July 5, 1958, p. 15w.

______ , "Hugh Neek — Then Nedlo the Gypsy Violinist," *Liverpool Echo*, July 19, 1958, p. 15.

Lewisohn, Mark. *Radio Times Guide to TV Comedy*. London: BBC, 1988.

Logan, Brian, "A Right Laugh: Geoff Northcott, the Standup Who Turned Tory," *The Guardian*, May 15, 2017, www.theguardian.com.

Mahoney, Con, "Ted Ray," *The Stage*, November 17, 1997, p. 15.

Marriott, R.B., "Royal Variety Supplement," *The Stage*, November 6, 1952, p. 6.

McKay, Mark, "Performers: Ted Ray," *Laugh Magazine*, No. 23, 2002, *http://laughterlog.com/2009/03/09/performers-tedray/ (accessed August 2020)*.

Mooney, John, "All Dead But Still Alive, the Comedians Who Kept Us Laughing," *https:/sluggerotoole.com/2019/12/04/comedians/* (accessed November 2021).

Newley, Patrick, "Andrew Ray," *Daily Express*, August 29, 2003, *http://andrewray.org.uk/obituaries/daily-express/* (accessed August 2020).

Norden, Denis. *Clips from Life*. London: Fourth Estate, 2008.

Olden, Mark, "Andrew Ray," *The Oldie*, March 2012, *http://andrewray.org.uk/from-the-vaults/father-and-son//* (accessed July 2020).

Owen, Maureen, "The Year Between…," *Evening Standard*, August 27, 1959, p. 8.

Owen, Michael, "Ted Ray, the King of the Wisecrack, Is Dead," *Evening Standard*, November 8, 1977, p. 3.

Pearce, Emery, "Any Favorite," *Daily Herald*, May 5, 1950, p. 6.

______ , "TV Demands Too Much," *Daily Herald*, May 15, 1952, p. 4.

Phillips, Philip, "May Quit TV," *Daily Herald*, January 14, 1952, p. 2.

______ , "Andrew Will Give TV Tips to Dad," *Daily Herald*, May 14, 1955, p. 4.

Porter, Henry, "Humour Sparkled for Fifty Years," *Liverpool Echo*, November 8, 1977, p. 5.

Ray, Ted. *Raising the Laughs*. London: Werner Laurie, 1952.

______ . *My Turn Next: A Book for Happy Tipplers*. London: Museum Press, 1963.

______ . *Golf — My Slice of Life*. London: W.H. Allan, 1972.

Raynor, Henry, "Laughing at Life with Ted Ray, *The Times*, August 29, 1967, p. 5.

Rees, Nigel. *My Radio Times*. London: CreateSpace Independent Publishing Platform, Scotts Valley, California: 2013.

Richards, Horace, "Ay Thang Yow!," *Woman's Own*, date unknown.

"The Serious Side of Being Funny," *The Times*, October 25, 1977, p. 12.

"Soaring Salaries of British Vaude Acts Worry Bookers; Some Up 100%," *Variety*, March 14, 1945, p. 46.

"Steam Radio…I Love It Says Ted Ray," source unidentified.

Smurthwaite, Nick, "Radio Sunshine," *The Stage*, March 17, 2005, p. 20.

"Ted Ray Is Thinking Up Some New Characters," *Sunday Mirror*, January 15, 1950, p. 1950.

"Ted Ray Tells the Difference," *The Stage*, August 11, 1949, p. 3.

"The Ted Ray Way to the Top," *Daily Herald*, September 25, 1952, p. 8.

Todd, Andrew. *Crews Hill: The Story of a Golf Club* (1916-1991). Barnet, U.K.: CB Printing Services, undated.

Took, Barry. *Laughter in the Air: An Informal History of British Radio Comedy*. London: Robson Books, 1981.

Usher, Shaun, "Ted Ray Dies on the Brink of a Comeback," *Daily Mail*, November 9, 1977, p. 19.

Vallance, Tom, "Andrew Ray," *The Independent*, August 26, 2003, *https://www.independent.co.uk/news/obituaries/andrew-ray-38999.html*. (accessed August 2020).

Wearing, J.P. *The London Stage 1930-1939: A Calendar of Plays and Players*. Metuchen, N.J.: Scarecrow Press, 1990.

______. *The London Stage 1940-1949: A Calendar of Plays and Players*. Metuchen, N.J.: Scarecrow Press, 1991.

Whitfield, June. *…and June Whitfield: The Autobiography*. London: Bantam Press, 2000.

Whittington-Egan, Richard, "All Roads Lead to the Pier Head," *The Times*, February 10, 1958, p. 3.

Williams, Bryn. *Red Tails in the Sunset*. Bicester, United Kingdon: Bound Biographies, 2006.

Williams, Kenneth. *Just Williams: An Autobiography*. London: J.M. Dent, 1985.

INDEX

WAKE UP AT THE BACK THERE!
It's JIMMY EDWARDS
ANTHONY SLIDE

I Thank You,
THE ARTHUR ASKEY STORY
ANTHONY SLIDE

Proudly hailing from Birmingham, England, ANTHONY SLIDE is the author or editor of more than 200 books on the history of popular entertainment, published over the past fifty and more years. His best known volumes include *Early American Cinema, The Films of D.W. Griffith, The Encyclopedia of Vaudeville, The Silent Feminists, Nitrate Won't Wait: A History of Film Preservation in the United States, Ravished Armenia and the Story of Aurora Mardiganian, Inside the Hollywood Fan Magazine: A History of Star Makers, Fabricators, and Gossip Mongers, Hollywood Unknowns: A History of Extras, Bit Players, and Stand-Ins, "It's the Pictures That Got Small": Charles Brackett on Billy Wilder and Hollywood's Golden Age,* and *Magnificent Obsession: The Outrageous History of Film Buffs, Collectors, Scholars, and Fanatics.* He has rightly been described by the *Los Angeles Times* as "a one-man publishing phenomenon."

In 1990, he was awarded a honorary doctorate of letters by Bowling Green University, and at that time he was described by Lillian Gish as "our pre-eminent historian of the silent film."

In more recent years, Anthony Slide has provided audio commentaries for many of Kino-Lorber's Blu Ray releases, and he also continues with his work as an appraiser of entertainment memorabilia, for which he is widely known.

Just a Regular Bloke: The Ted Ray Story is the third volume documenting the work of British comedians, with the previous two books being *Wake Up at the Back There!: It's Jimmy Edwards* and *I Thank You: The Arthur Askey Story.*